HAITI
ONCE AGAIN

...You were bought at a price,
do not become slaves of human beings...
1 Corinthians 7:23

J.R. Gelin

PRESS

Table of Contents

Introduction

As you read through the pages of this book, you will find elements
and concepts from disciplines as varied as modern history,
biblical theology, and even some aspects of science and molecular
genetics. It is my understanding that it takes all of that, and more, to
understand Haiti both as a country and as a symbol of liberty.

As a country, the Republic of Haiti is located in the Caribbean Sea
and has a total land area of 27,750 square kilometers (10,714 square
miles). There are roughly 9 million Haitians in the world, with about 1
million living overseas in what has been called the Haitian Diaspora.
The Republic of Haiti shares the island of Haiti with the Dominican
Republic which occupies roughly two thirds of the island with a total
land area of 48,442 square kilometers (18,704 square miles).

As a symbol, however, the Republic of Haiti represents the
never ending struggle for human freedom, liberty and dignity. Since
declaring its independence from France in 1804, Haiti has been
fighting for its survival, not only because of its own internal contradictions but more importantly due to fierce international pressure
and opposition. Whereas Haiti can be seen as the mother of liberty
for people of African descent and virtually of all Latin America, the

country, nevertheless, has received excessively bad press and has also been invaded many times.

In the United Sates, Haitians were targeted quite unfairly as a high risk group for AIDS when the disease was first discovered in the country some 30 years ago. More recently, a scientific article attempted to portray Haiti as a key point of distribution of the AIDS virus, even though the first cases recorded in Europe very early at the onset of the epidemic had no connection with Haiti whatsoever, and direct links to Central Africa where the disease apparently was first discovered were established.

The country has also been vilified on the religious and theological front. The success of the Haitian Revolution has been attributed to a so-called spiritual pact with the Devil by a few American televangelists with large audience. The direct corollary to this message is that the God of heaven has put a curse on the nation and people of Haiti so they could not prosper. And as would be expected, this erroneous view took a life of its own and has corrupted the message of Jesus Christ that's available in the pages of the New Testament.

As Haiti changed the world 200 years ago in the context of colonialism and slavery, the country can once again make life better for its people – this time, in the context of globalization. If you have ever asked yourself why Haiti seems to be a magnet for disasters, natural or man-made, I think you may find a few answers in the pages of this book. If not, I promise you will at least have a different view of the country.

Chapter 1
A VERY UN-HAPPY BICENTENARY

History records that three great revolutions have changed the face of the world during the last 300 years. In chronological order, the first one was the American Revolution that culminated in the independence of the United States from England in 1776. A little over a decade later, the French Revolution started with the fall of the Bastille in 1789. Last, but not least, the Haitian Revolution gave birth to the nation of Haiti in 1804.

One of the main reasons the British colonies in America wanted to become independent was to stay away from the heavy taxes they were forced to pay to the European power. Although many had originally fled Europe and come to America for more religious liberty, those who had settled in the new country had developed rich and prosperous colonies based on slavery. Africans were kidnapped in the original countries and sold as properties for free labor in the new world. When the United States gained its political independence from the United Kingdom, the revolution meant that all the wealth extracted from the slave labor would remain in the new country and no longer be shared with England. Essentially, and at least in its very beginning, the American Revolution was merely a political and economic separation from the British.

In the case of France, one major consequence of the storming of the Bastille was the end of the socio-political structure that had kept most of the population under control by the various Kings who had ruled the country. Incidentally, King Louis XVI was beheaded in 1793, just a few years after the start of the revolution; but the fate of the French colonies in the new world had not changed. Africans and their descendants were still held as slaves in the Caribbean islands and whatever was produced in these colonies was first and foremost for the benefit of France. Essentially, and much like the American Revolution, the French Revolution started as a system change for the benefit of French citizens and had not much to do with the French colonies.

What took place in Haiti, however, was entirely different. Whereas both the American Revolution in 1776 and the French Revolution 1789 were primarily against monarchy and its privileges, there was no change in sight for the millions of African men, women and children who were being raped, tortured, terrorized, beaten, burned to death, or buried alive day after day on the various hellish plantations of the New world. It took the Haitian Revolution to put an end to that system and bring about generalized freedom for all, regardless of ethnicity or country of origin – starting on the island itself.

Compared to the American Revolution and the French Revolution put together, the Haitian Revolution literally changed the face of the

New world, and accomplished something much deeper and more significant for mankind. The success of the Haitian Revolution meant that from that point on there was a place in the new world where every human being was free from all sorts of bondage, especially people of African descent who had been denied their human dignity and basic rights for three centuries. When we consider the very deep implications of these three great revolutions for the Western World in particular, and for mankind in general, it is not difficult to see why the bicentenary of each came as a great event of international significance. Let us have a brief review here:

1.   When the United States celebrated its 200th year of independence and existence in 1976, people came from around the world to participate in this great event. There was, for example, a fleet of boats sailing from different nations and arriving in the port of New York City (1) with jubilant tourists. Special coins were issued for the occasion and cultural events took place throughout the country. Although the cold war was going on, the celebration of the American bicentenary was a great success and neither the Soviet Union nor any other communist country made a visible move to crash the party, so to speak. It was a great celebration.

2.   In 1989, Paris received people from many countries to participate in the great festivities of its bicentenary. France was also the place chosen for the G7 International Summit, a meeting of the seven leading industrial democracies, and several

international political figures attended the celebrations. There was some unease on the part of political opponents of French President François Mitterrand, and as reported by the BBC (2) some trouble-makers fought in the streets of Paris and harassed foreign TV crews while others threw stones at law enforcement officers. However, there was no political aggression against Paris, and at the end of the day the bicentennial celebration in France was a great success.

3. Now, when it comes to Haiti's attempt to celebrate its own bicentenary, the picture is entirely different. Naturally, Haiti expected people, organizations and foreign governments from around the world to come and celebrate with the first black republic. French writer Claude Ribbe reports that France in particular initiated a big campaign both in Haiti and in Africa to prevent a successful Haiti-Africa connection during the bicentennial celebrations (3). Ultimately, only the President of South Africa, Thabo Mbeki, made the long trip from the ancient continent to represent his own country. Some officials from the United States and the Caribbean participated, and other small delegations came from Africa but for cultural reasons and not as political representatives of their countries. There was also a magnification of political disturbances coming from the people who opposed the government of that time. But the most tragic part of this episode came when American and French soldiers jointly invaded the country,

removed the government and appointed a provisional group of their choice. United Nations troops joined the party and initiated a military occupation of the country on its 200th anniversary-the same year chosen by the United Nations to commemorate the abolition of slavery.

At the end of the 18th century, political events in the United States, France and Haiti collided to determine a new order of things in the Western world; and in the first decade of the 21st century the three countries met together in the land of Dessalines, but under very peculiar circumstances. In 1976, the United States had a successful bicentenary. In 1989, France had a successful bicentenary. In 2004, Haiti had a very *UN*-happy bicentenary and the country continues to suffer all sorts of damage from the tragic and violent disruption of its rightful celebration.

But, in reality, the desecration of Haiti's bicentennial should not be a surprise to anyone familiar with the long and tumultuous path the people of Haiti has had to take for their journey. We will look at some of these main obstacles in the next chapters.

Chapter 2
The First Encounter

When Christopher Columbus came upon Haiti for the first time on December 5, 1492, the island was already inhabited by five nations of native people, and it also had a name. The original name was Haiti and it means land of mountains in the native language, which corresponds greatly to its topography. The first encounter between the Europeans and the native Haitians at the end of the 15th century was a culture shock and a cause for great surprise and amazement to both parties.

Columbus and his crew were amazed by the beauty of the island and as well as the lifestyle and philosophy of the natives; and for some reason, he thought the entire region was somehow not too far from the Garden of Eden mentioned in the Book of Genesis. The Spaniards who came to Haiti were European Catholics and were most likely familiar with the 10th commandment:

You shall not covet your neighbor's house. You shall not covet your neighbor's wife, or his male or female servant, his ox or donkey, or anything that belongs to your neighbor." (Genesis 20:17)

Nevertheless, they claimed everything they saw for Spain, and after deciding to call the island Hispaniola (the Spanish island), they referred to one northern section as Valparaiso (valley of paradise) on account of its natural beauty. Through his initial interactions with the native Haitians, Columbus noted that at first he was not able to know whether they held any personal property because apparently everything they had was shared with all; and this way of living in relation to the material world was puzzling to him as it was the opposite of the European mindset that was more about obtaining material wealth than about living life itself. Here are a few words from Columbus cited by Meltzer (4):

...Anything they have, if it be asked for they never say no, but rather invite the person to accept it, and show as much lovingness as though they would give their hearts...Nor have I ever been able to learn whether they held personal property, for it seemed to me that whatever one had, they all took shares of...

But if Columbus knew and understood his Bible at all, he would have remembered a similar attitude exemplified by the members in the original church that Jesus Christ built and established in Jerusalem:

All the believers were one in heart and mind. No one claimed that any of their possessions was their own, but they shared everything they had. With great power the apostles continued to testify to the resurrection of the Lord Jesus. And God's grace was so powerfully at work in them all that there were no needy persons among them. For from time to time those who owned

7

land or houses sold them, brought the money from the sales and put it at the apostles' feet, and it was distributed to anyone who had need. Joseph, a Levite from Cyprus, whom the apostles called Barnabas (which means "son of encouragement"), sold a field he owned and brought the money and put it at the apostles' feet. (Acts 4:32-37)

Evidently, Columbus and his crew failed to see the similarities as they were blinded by their own agenda, greediness, and drive for success - whatever success could mean at that time. We know through history that the European mindset succeeded in crushing the native societies and getting everything it was possible to get out of them, until another generation put an end to it.

However, to understand what happened in Haiti from 1492 to 1804, one cannot neglect the religious views of the main actors. Religion has played and continues to play a critical role in shaping and reshaping life on the island, still today. I will return to this point later but for now, let us take a look at the religious background of the people who showed up in the three boats that first week of December 1492.

In 15th century Europe, Spain and Portugal were the leaders of naval exploration with the Portuguese having the advantage of previous successful voyages in Africa and Asia. Pope Alexander VI had worked with the Spanish and Portuguese crowns to divide the new world to be found from future voyages between the two of them. But there are two key historical elements that can help to better describe the political and religious climate of that time:

- In 1492, Spain was purging itself of its Jewish population by a royal edict requiring all Jews present in the kingdom to embrace Christianity (their version of it) or face dispossession, trials, and death if necessary. In fact, the voyage of Columbus was delayed by several weeks because he had to wait for that wave of Jewish persecution to take effect before he could leave Spain (4).

- Prior to that anti-Semitic campaign in Spain, Europe was engaged in several crusades in the Holy Land that killed countless men, women, and children in the most horrific manner. Spain, in particular, had just launched the inquisition under the command of a certain catholic priest called Thomas Torquemada appointed by King Ferdinand and Queen Isabella. Torquemada was named Inquisitor-General in 1483 and as a result of his policies people accused of heresy were judged, sentenced, tortured and executed (5). Columbus and his men lived under that system.

No doubt, this political and religious atmosphere shaped the minds of the Spaniards who embarked in the three boats with a burning zeal to conquer new lands for their politico-religious system (faith and the kingdom) by any means necessary. Accordingly, when these 90 exhausted and very impatient men finally came before Haiti, they were ready for action in keeping with their long tradition of religious and political violence. And this attitude, this predisposition, or this mindset had absolutely nothing to do with the teachings that Jesus Christ left for his disciples to study and follow. Yes, these men called themselves Christians, and perhaps some of them may have even believed they were Christians, but their version of Christianity had no apparent connection neither with the Christ himself nor with the first Christian church he had established.

I think it is critically important here to draw the contrast between the recorded life of Jesus Christ with his disciples and the historical records covering Columbus with his crew. Whereas Columbus and his men got out of their boats to conquer, destroy, steal and kill, the Scriptures present a different scenario whenever Jesus or his disciples got out of a boat to meet with people. Let us look at a couple of examples found in the New Testament:

1. According to the book of Mark Chapter 5, Jesus came out of a boat and healed a man who was demon possessed, and he left the area right after this great miracle because the people asked him to go; Jesus was there to save and serve and as a result did not hurt nor curse anyone. Jesus was after the well-being of the man himself, and he was not after gold or other material possessions.

2. Years later, as recorded in the book of Acts Chapters 27 and 28, Paul and his companions also ended up on an island called Malta while they were traveling by boat; there, Paul prayed for the people and blessed them until it was time for him to

leave. Like Jesus before him, Paul was not after the gold and other material possessions of the islanders and his passage among them brought healing and comfort.

We certainly cannot say the same for Columbus and his men. Jesus Christ, the founder of the New Covenant, warned us all of upcoming wolves dressed in sheep's clothing (see Matthew 7:5), and he said a tree can be identified by the very fruits that it produces (see Matthew 7:20). The historical records show that the native Haitians were not enough to quench the thirst and greediness of the Spaniards and in just one decade it was time to import kidnapped Africans as replacements. Their fate would have been entirely different, had they been visited by Jesus or by some first century Christians!

Chapter 3
The African Presence

The first Africans arrived in Haiti – known then as Hispaniola – in 1503 as imported replacements to the dying Indians. This is what most people know and believe about the African presence in the new world. It is true that as enslaved people Africans came to the island at the start of the 16th century, but black people and African culture were already present in the new world long before Columbus and his men set foot on Caribbean soil in 1492. The evidence to support the pre-Columbian African presence in the new world relies on both direct observations and archeological findings.

As an example of direct observation, Columbus and other Spanish explorers reported about various settlements of black people found in Central and South America, as discussed below by Legrand H. Clegg II (6):

> *The best evidence of the Black presence in America before Columbus comes from the pen of the "great discoverer" himself. In his Journal of the Second Voyage, Columbus reported that when he reached Haiti the native Americans told him that black-skinned people had come from the south and southeast in boats,*

trading in gold-tipped medal spears. At least a dozen other European explorers, including Vasco Nunez de Balboa, also reported seeing or hearing of "Negroes" when they reached the New world.

Specifically, there was one black tribe known as The Caribs described as dark-skinned warriors with a very characteristic hairdo: on one side of their head their hair streamed down in long braids whereas on the opposite side it was shaven clean (4). It is quite interesting that the word Caribbean itself is derived from the name of these black tribes living in the new world, long before Columbus was even conceived in his mother's womb. In a very practical sense, whenever we use the word Caribbean today to refer to that specific section of the American continent we are in essence talking about pre-Columbian Black presence in the new world, which in itself is an element of the rich African legacy.

When it comes to archeological evidence that supports the pre-Columbian African presence on the American continent, the bulk of it lies in the countries of Mexico and Columbia primarily in two forms:

1. First, there are several gigantic monuments dating hundreds or thousands of years before Columbus. We are all familiar with the Aztecs and what they left behind, but centuries before the Aztec civilization in Mexico, the land was occupied by the Olmec people who developed a relatively sophisticated culture. In particular, their civilization left behind both figurines and colossal heads carved in stone and that exhibit

clear Black or Ethiopian features. In ancient cultures, gigantic heads in general would indicate some form of reverence to individuals who held leadership positions and roles in these civilizations (7).

2.   Second, uncovered and translated scripts from the Olmec civilization show they spoke the Mende language which itself was used in Western Africa. Certainly, no one would make the bold claim that the Olmec people left the American continent to go spread their culture all the way to Africa. Rather, the opposite seems logical, meaning that people from the African continent came to America a long time before Columbus and left behind evidence of their presence and culture (8, 9). In addition, the types of calendars and pyramids found in Mexico appear to point to the African connection (10). This would explain how such distinctly African cultural elements such as mummification and construction of pyramids are found in so many parts of Latin America.

Even without these types of hard evidence, it is not diffi-cult really to understand how ancient Africans could have sailed directly to the various parts of the American continent. Not only is the distance relatively short, but the ancient African kingdoms were very prosperous and advanced especially Ghana and Mali to name a few. The Bible in particular states that Moses, who basically founded the nation of Israel, was educated in all the wisdom of the Egyptians (see Acts 7:22). We know also that Columbus spent some time in Africa and his connections with Portugal could have easily exposed him to African tales about dry lands beyond the oceans. Many people agree that Columbus did not really discover America *sensu stricto*, but he simply was the first recorded European traveler to arrive there in 1492. In that context, the phrase new world itself has meaning for European explorers relative to their knowledge of the world at that time only.

The first enslaved Africans came to Haiti in 1503 and from that point in time slave cargos were regularly delivered to the island year after year, while families were being broken as members were sold to different owners depending on market needs and fluctuations. But it is also quite interesting, from a purely historical point to view, to realize that exactly 300 years later, the last cargo of French troops led by French General Rochambeau slowly moved out of Haiti in 1803 to return to France – beaten, humiliated, weak, sick, and utterly amazed at Dessalines. It took 300 years for the cruel system to collapse in Haiti, but the country is facing new struggles in the context of globalization in the 21st century. Yet, positive changes can happen in Haiti once again.

Chapter 4
The Beginning of the End

After the first enslaved Africans were brought to the island in 1503, slavery continued on the island but not without tensions, and not as smoothly as the plantation owners would have liked it to be. Because it is unnatural for one man to own another man, any society based on such a model simply cannot exist for too long. Naturally, in Hispaniola/Saint-Domingue, it was only a matter of time before the whole system would explode. Internal contradictions in the colony and acts of revolt by the slaves amplified continually until a widespread revolt broke out in 1791.

In the decade following the general revolt of the slaves (1791-1081), Toussaint Louverture defeated the British and the Spanish troops separately, and he used his military and political genius to unite the entire island as one single French colony under the name Saint-Domingue. Because of Toussaint, the British had completely abandoned their hope of having a portion of the island, and the defeated Spanish army did not make any new attempt at regaining control. The end of British aspirations and Spanish control marked, in some way, the beginning of the end of colonization and slavery on the island, and by extension in the new world.

By the time Toussaint published the 1801 Constitution there was no question in anybody's mind as to who was in charge of the entire colony or what the name of the island was. Toussaint Louverture was its Governor, Roman Catholicism was its official religion, and as we can see in Article 1 of the 1801 Constitution, the entire island was a French colony known as Saint-Domingue (11):

Saint-Domingue in its entire expanse, and Samana, La Tortue, La Gonave, Les Cayemites, L'Ile-a-Vache, La Saone and other adjacent islands form the territory of a single colony, which is part of the French Empire, but ruled under particular laws.

Form a purely historical point of view we can see that Toussaint abolished Hispaniola at the end of the 18th century to expand Saint-Domingue. No longer was there any talk of Hispaniola because the Spaniards had lost the colony to France thanks to the general revolt of the slaves and the vision and leadership of Toussaint. A few short years later, Jean Jacques Dessalines gave the final blow to the colonial system by abolishing Saint-Domingue altogether to give birth to Haiti on January 1st, 1804. The official declaration of independence was made in the city of Gonaives, and here is how Article 1 of the new constitution put it (12):

The people inhabiting the island formerly called St. Domingo, hereby agree to form themselves into a free state sovereign and

17

independent of any other power in the universe, under the name of empire of Hayti.

From that point on, it was no longer a question of Hispaniola or of Saint-Domingue but of Haiti. There was no more room for Spanish rule or French laws. A brave, free and independent nation has taken control of its destiny and has chosen to restore the original and pre-colonial name of the island: Haiti. The inhabitants of that free and independent nation were known as Haitians, not Hispaniolans or Saint-Dominguois. One can say that both legally and politically, the words Hispaniola and Saint-Domingue had no more meaning or value in the Caribbean. Interestingly enough, when the Spanish speaking portion of the island population decided to break away and form a different country in 1844, they got their independence not from Spain and not France but directly from Haiti. Still today, the Dominican Republic continues to celebrate its independence from Haiti.

After the great success of the Haitian Revolution in 1804, Dessalines did not keep the French colonial name of Saint-Domingue, or the Spanish colonial name of Hispaniola. Instead he went back over 300 years of bloody and painful history to pick up the original name of the island. His choice of name has both a natural meaning (Haiti means land of mountains in Taino language) and a profoundly political meaning (colonization is over, slavery is over, European rule is over). From a political and historical point of view, the Island of Haiti is occupied today by the Republic of Haiti and the Dominican Republic.

When we see the colonial name Hispaniola being used routinely today by the international press to refer to the Island of Haiti, this choice of word conveys the idea of colonialism and disregards the success of the Haitian Revolution. I believe it makes perfect sense to use the name Island of Haiti instead of Hispaniola in order a) to follow the Dessalinian logic, b) to keep his heritage alive, c) to honor and respect the Haitian Revolution, and d) to celebrate the memory of the native Haitians who were enslaved and massacred by the Spaniards.

And this would not create any confusion at all as similar situations exist in other parts of the world. People routinely talk about New York whether they mean New York City or other places in the state of New York; there is no confusion there, so there should not be any in the case of Haiti. Also, People talk about Mexico and just clarify if they mean Mexico City or some other place in the country of Mexico; there is no confusion there, so there should not be any when it comes to Haiti. The same can be said for Panama City and the country of Panama, Singapore and Singapore, Luxembourg and Luxembourg, Kuwait and Kuwait City, Djibouti and Djibouti, or Guatemala and Guatemala City. It should not be difficult for people to talk about Haiti as the island and just clarify if they mean the Republic of Haiti or neighboring Dominican Republic.

Chapter 5
The Beauty and Power of 1804

The declaration of Haiti's independence from France on January 1, 1804 was met with great and untold excitement throughout the country. It was a very beautiful scene to see thousands of men, women and children, who only months ago were in hiding or running for their very lives, come out rejoicing to join the bands of the victorious indigenous army. There was no more a master to fear or to obey, the physical and mental shackles had been removed, and every citizen was now free regardless of ethnicity or gender.

The birth of Haiti made it possible for people who were once enslaved and subjugated to begin the process of their own development and self-realization, in the Caribbean first and then in the rest of the Americas. This bold step toward self-determination appears to correspond to a universal desire in all of us humans, as outlined by Sankatsing (13):

In nature, as well as in history, there is a cosmic desire to survive, to grow, to flourish, to bear fruit and to defeat death by reproduction. That force is what is called development. The history of the Americas and the Caribbean should be understood as the

clash between two opposing processes: envelopment, a model-
ling from outside, and development, commanded by the inner
clock; in other words, a clash between forces of subjugation and
imitation versus forces of creation and selfrealization.

The leaders of the new country also understood the magnitude of their responsibilities with regards to this unparalleled accomplishment. Dessalines initiated a massive campaign of restoration throughout the country in order not only to rebuild what had been destroyed during the savage war of independence, but also to start new projects aimed at protecting and defending the integrity of the nation. Roads were being repaired, school and church buildings were under construction or renovation, and throughout the land fortresses were rising up with an architecture that amazes tourists until today.

The first few decades after 1804 also saw the birth and rise of Haitian literature, as the country was moving along on the road to creation and self-realization. Bulletins, journals, newsletters and magazines came into existence in many parts of the country. The subjects explored included political ideas, Haitian sovereignty, human dignity and freedom, or just simple poetry (14). Great literary documents and masterpieces were produced by internationally famous authors and scientists such as Anténor Firmin and Louis Joseph Janvier. It was Anténor Firmin who wrote the great book entitled '*De l'égalité des Races Humaines*'. This masterpiece of more than 600 pages was published in Paris in 1885 to counter another book that sought to establish the idea of innate inequalities among the various human races, as understood by some people of that era.

Famous poets and novelists of the first few decades of Haitian literature include Emeric Bergeaud, Oswald Durand, and Frédéric Marcelin just to name a few. Some poets were writing about the beauty of the country while others had their eyes on the people of the land. In the early years pieces of writing were produced mostly in French, although the famous poem '*Choucoune*' was published in Haitian Creole by Oswald Durand in 1883. As the country was seeking to project its image to the outside world, the language of Voltaire was the best vehicle available at that time. Many poets and novelists were also expressing a connection not only to the language of France but also to its culture as a whole.

Towards the middle of the 20th century, however, a new school of thought began to emerge with a focus on African culture and philosophy. With the publication in 1928 of the famous book entitled '*Ainsi Parla l'Oncle*' by Dr. Jean Price Mars, a new era of Haitian literature had definitely started, the era of Negritude. Later on in 1944, Jacques Roumain published '*Les Gouverneurs de la Rosée*' which was turned into a great movie played by a cast of Haitian actors. The debate between members of the Indigenous School and those who wanted a cultural connection with France contributed greatly to the progress and diversity of Haitian literature.

At the same time, the country was also searching for itself politically, especially in the context of aggression from other countries including Germany. When the American marines landed in Port-au-Prince on July 28, 1915 to begin a military occupation that would last 19 years, Haitian literature was also impacted. This impact was greatly amplified as elements of indigenous art, some dating from the native civilizations, were being either destroyed or collected to be brought to the Unites States. People reacted to this in several ways, and one such movement that sought to rescue this part of the land's heritage resulted in the creation of the Ethnology Bureau, which later became part of the State University as Faculté d'Ethnologie.

The push on the part of some brilliant intellectuals to return to the African roots of the Haitian people focused not only on cultural elements but also of the religion of Vodou. Famous Haitian poet Carl Brouard, disillusioned and outraged by the sufferings of the masses and the abuses caused by the elite, urged people to begin honoring central elements of the Vodou religion such as the drum and the bell. There were campaigns of persecution against Vodou under the name of anti-superstition efforts, and, interestingly enough, the Church of God was also shut down for two years in the country (August 12, 1941 – August 13, 1943) by the government of Elie Lescot, under several charges including suspected communist affiliations (15)!

Vodou, practiced at that time almost exclusively by people living outside of or on the fringes of the cities (*en dehors*), began to receive some positive review throughout the country. This sort of ascension has produced, among other things, a new genre of popular music called Mizik Rasin (Roots Music) starting mainly in the 1980's, which is different from the popular genre called Konpa. In French or in Haitian Creole, people continue to write for or against Vodou, discussing practices such as zombification or the various obscure and secret groups that seek to control the night in the countryside. Many have tried to paint Vodou as THE culture of the Haitian people instead of what it really is, a simple element of that rich and varied culture.

In the beginning of the 20th century, a few more people started writing short texts in Haitian Creole. One of these early documents is a 1928 translation of the Gospel of John from French into Haitian Creole by a French missionary called Elie Marc (16). Pastor Marc married a Haitian woman in the North and continued his mission-ary work there. Some have argued that political independence is followed naturally by cultural independence expressed in language, music, and religious traditions. Unfortunately, some of Haiti's Christian leaders are not yet reached complete theological indepen-dence, which is required to maximize the relevance of the indig-enous church in the country.

Non-Haitians were also in awe of the new nation that came out of the first and only known successful slave revolution in history. Many writers from Europe for example came to Haiti to see the country and its people with their own eyes, and some wrote reports and books on Haiti as the Black Kingdom or the Black Republic. Whereas in France, in particular, several of the people who had been defeated either by Toussaint or by Dessalines were forced to defend themselves against the countrymen, some British observers were praising the leaders of the Haitian Revolution for their philosophy and political achievements.

One direct consequence of 1804 in the first decades of the 19th century was the definitive crushing of the widespread myth of black innate inferiority. While people of African descent were still being held in slavery in the United States or being discriminated against elsewhere in the new world, Haitian officials were proudly representing their country internationally.

Chapter 6
The Litany of Violence

An online article published by BBC News on January 2012 reports that the country of Mexico has recorded 47,515 drugs-related killings in just the last five years. This number corresponds to an average of 9,503 per year or 791.9 per month, which gives an approximate number of 26.4 killings every single day or roughly 1 killing per hour. This carnage has been going on for five consecutive years in a country that shares close to 2,000 miles of border with the United States (17, 18).

The number of murders connected to what has been called Mexico's Drugs War would be enough to wipe out an entire small town in rural America or Canada. If any country would be in need of a mission of stabilization like the one controlling Haiti since 2004, it sure looks like Mexico. Yet, with widespread violence and all these killings taking place on a daily basis just across the American southern border, we do not see any special military mission from the United Nations flying to the rescue of these unfortunate and defenseless Mexican families. Perhaps, one will have to wait a few more years as it may not be as easy for foreign troops to get into Mexico as it is for Haiti.

I mentioned the on-going war in Mexico here to establish the regional context of international reporting on Haiti with regard to crimes and violence. Anyone who had paid attention to the coverage Haiti has received recently, especially in the aftermath of the 2010 earthquake, would agree that many times the sound bites coming from some foreign journalists could almost be likened to the lyrics of some chant or religious litany about violent crimes. Violence was oftentimes anticipated even without any reasonable basis for a particular situation. And whenever violent acts could be recorded, whatever their immediate or ultimate cause, such acts were likely to be magnified as to fit some concealed mental or ideological framework. But the truth of the matter is that there is a big difference between the reality of violence in Haiti and the perception created by international media coverage.

When the numbers of homicides and other crimes were put together for various countries in a recent study, it was found that Haiti was far from the top for violence, which would indicate the disparity between reality and perception for that matter. According to a report published in 2008, Haiti registered about 5.6 murders per 100,000 people compared to a Caribbean average of 30 per 100,000 people (19). These numbers have prompted some observers to refer to the widespread association of the country with violence as a '*big myth*'. And based on the statistics alone, some have said that in

27

reality Haiti is much safer than the media coverage would suggest (20).

Additionally, the atmosphere of violence that has been reported after amplification can be connected to the country's political system, which in turn is strongly influenced by international players. And generally speaking, life is normal outside of Port-au-Prince with occasional crimes that would be expected in any other society. In the *2011 Global Study of Homicide* released by the United Nations, there was nothing strikingly singular about Haiti to justify the image that has been created by the constant effort to inject the word violence at the earliest opportunity in any report about the country (21).

Perhaps the best illustration of this obsession with a violent Haiti is the recent report posted by a journalist who claimed that after visiting Haiti she could not process the thought of sex without associating it with violence (22). And what would be the reason for her mental shock? Apparently, she interacted with a Haitian woman who was a victim of gang rape in Port-au-Prince. According to that journalist, not only was sex and violence irremediably associated in her mind as a result of that encounter, but also stress and fear were the only two things that held her together after she returned home to the United States from Haiti. She continued her story and explained that her road to mental recovery led her to solicit and obtain violent sex from an old boy friend. In her fractured mind, that was the only way she could recover.

Other journalists reacted to this story (23), but this is one tiny example of the challenges Haiti is facing and has been dealing with since its birth. I want to conclude the litany of violence with a few words from a resident of Port-au-Prince quoted in a 2008 report (19):

'Our problem isn't violence,' said Yvner Meneide, a Port-au-Prince artisan. 'If we were violent, we would organise demonstrations every day, we would be destroying things. But Haitian people are very moderate. We might be hungry, but we are calm.'

Haiti needs to write her own story, once again!

Chapter 7
The AIDS Stigma

In 2010, Cholera was reported in Haiti and in one year it had killed around 6,000 people and infected more than 400,000 (24). Previously absent in the country, the disease was found to be imported and connected with a battalion of UN soldiers from the country of Nepal – a place where a recent outbreak was recorded (25).

Haiti is no position currently to request and obtain compensations for the people affected since the country is under military occupation. But I suspect that a few years from now, a small group of experts somewhere may try to rewrite the narrative in an effort to 'show' that the disease was already present in the country – contrary to the known and observed facts of this case. It is my opinion that something similar happened to Haiti concerning HIV/AIDS.

AIDS stands for Acquired Immuno-Deficiency Syndrome and describes a very wide range of symptoms that can affect the body and mind of people infected with the causing virus. Due to the breakdown of the immune system of affected patients, all sorts of infectious diseases develop and can result in death. It is estimated that this disease alone has killed roughly 30 million people world-wide since it was first discovered about 30 years ago (26).

By most accounts, the explosion of AIDS in humans started in central Africa in the 1970's, regardless of how the virus itself entered the bloodstream of the first infected people. From there it spread directly to Europe, particularly to Denmark and France. The case of a Danish doctor who was treating patients in Africa was recorded as very puzzling to her care givers in Europe after she returned home for her final days and nobody could find the exact cause for her slow death. She slowly wasted away and ultimately died on December 12, 1977. Around the same time, the mysterious disease appeared also in Paris with unexplained cases of infected people from Portugal, Zaire, Congo (1, 27).

Today we know that AIDS is caused by a retrovirus called HIV (Human Immunodeficiency Virus), but at the onset of the epidemic no one even knew what the new disease was, let alone its cause. In an atmosphere of ignorance coupled with hysteria, people began to propose all sorts of names to describe the syndrome while the virus itself was being propagated freely and rapidly through sexual activities, the use of infected needles, and even blood transfusion across the United States and Europe.

For example, the name GRID (Gay Related Immune Deficiency) was proposed by some scientists because they noticed that in the United States in particular, the disease was primarily found in gay men living in San Francisco and New York City. There is evidence

31

that one single gay man from Canada named Gaëtan Dugas, who worked as a flight attendant with Air Canada, played an enormous role in spreading the virus around the globe. Gaëtan traveled frequently to the United States, Europe and the Caribbean, he was extremely promiscuous and continued his sexual activities even after he knew he knew he was infected. He was referred to as 'Patient Zero' in the early attempts to pinpoint the cause and propagation of the disease because scientists at that time could clearly see his footprints in numerous cases everywhere (1, 27).

But, as AIDS began to be found outside the gay community and affect people of all walks of life, new acronyms were proposed to identify at risk groups. When symptoms were found in a few Haitian men living in the United States, the name 4H was put forward to single out Homosexuals, Hemophiliacs, Heroin addicts, and (of course) Haitians, even though the disease was found in people who did not fall in any of these groups. There were at that time an estimated 150, 000 Haitians immigrants in the Miami area and 350,000 in and around New York.

Haitian-Americans reacted strongly against this very negative stereotype, and rightfully so. Despite the increasing number of gay men in San Francisco diagnosed with the disease, San Franciscans in general were never portrayed as an at-risk group; and the same can be said for New York City where many cases were found. In 1990, Haitian-Americans marched in New York to protest against the offense, and Haitian artists such as Ansy Dérose and TiManno composed and released special songs on the subject. Ultimately, Haitians were removed from the list, but the AIDS stigma created did not disappear as easily (28, 29).

Haitians thought this outrage was behind them until a scientific article was published in 2007 claiming to establish with absolute certainty that the virus leaped from Africa to Haiti and from Haiti to the world (30). 'Patient Zero' is no longer Canadian flight attendant Gaëtan Dugas who was identified in the 1980's, but rather an imaginary single man who left Haiti, went to Africa, picked up the virus and then returned to Haiti with it. This story sounds more like a scientific fable than anything else, and after reading the paper I identified a few weaknesses and flaws that are listed below:

1. The authors started their study with blood samples that were over 20 years old. It is common knowledge in molecular genetics that genetic materials tend to degrade over time, and one consequence of poor quality DNA is the risk of getting erroneous results from analysis, which ultimately leads to erroneous conclusions. The authors knew this but they did their work anyway. Sure enough, one of their starting blood samples did not yield any usable products at all due most likely to deterioration because of age and storage conditions. This would seem to indicate that the other blood samples may have given products of questionable quality.

2. The authors also started with 6 blood samples, a very small sample size for such a study. They did not start 6,000 samples,

or 600, or even 60, but just 6 old blood samples out of which only 5 yielded some products. Again, it is common knowledge in science that sample size is critical in any valid study, especially when it comes to making meaningful inferences or deductions. How valid can any conclusion be when it's based on 5 samples? This reminds me of a classmate in high school who volunteered to be part of the racing team after explaining he finished third in the latest race he participated in from his previous school; when the principal asked him how many students took part in that race, his answer surprised everyone: 3 contestants! Yes, only three students ran and he finished third. Now we all understand that this 3rd place would have an entirely different meaning if the size of the running group was 500 or even 50 students. I see the same thing here with a study based on 5 blood samples collected over 20 years earlier; it does not have great value.

3.   The whole study was based on presumptions that, by their very nature and definition, cannot be assessed and proven beyond any doubt. I will mention only a couple of these presumptions here:

   a. The authors say that the five Haitian patients entered the United States after 1975 and progressed to AIDS by 1981 but were *'presumably'* infected with the virus before leaving Haiti. This cannot be proven and should be rejected as pure imagination. The five Haitian patients could as well have been infected after entering the United States because the virus was already present on American soil and even in Europe (27).

b. A critical and central presumption of the study is the idea that educated Haitians who went to Africa to help educate and administer the newly independent country of Zaire, for example, received the virus there and brought it back with them to Haiti where it would later spread and get into the bloodstream of unsuspecting American tourists. This idea is false on at least two counts: first the virus was already present in Europe and North America via direct contact with Africa, and people were already dying before its presence was detected in a few Haitian patients living in the United States; second, there is no evidence that some of the educated Haitians who went to Africa were infected at all and made the trip back to Haiti; in reality, many of these expatriates returned to the Caribbean nation only after the Duvalier dictatorship ended in 1986. As mentioned earlier, the one person who traveled throughout the world with the virus in his bloodstream was the Canadian flight attendant named Gaëtan Dugas, whom American scientists interviewed, examined and considered as 'Patient Zero' very early on

4.   Finally, I will point out that the authors exhibited a great deal of flexibility, improvisation and liberty in their approach, whether in choosing which DNA sequences to include in

their comparisons or in deciding what to report. For example, they mention that DNA fragments were sequenced twice but they do not give any comparison of the outcomes of these two distinct sequencing efforts; perhaps they found some great discrepancies and decided to keep moving anyway, or they could have found a perfect match between the two sets of sequence data but since this information is not presented the reader has no way of knowing. Ultimately, they found a 99.79% probability of their conclusion, which in itself is a very curious thing!

People familiar with academic life in North America understand the pressure scientists routinely face to publish new studies so they can advance their own career or receive new funding. This particular study was published in 2007, just a few months before world AIDS day (31) when people around the globe are typically encouraged to pay particular attention to this disease. The paper is likely to have generated some interest in the work of these authors, and such exposure would benefit them in more than one way.

In face of the very aggressive climate existing in the scientific community, particularly concerning early AIDS research in the United States, some French scientists were very uncomfortable with the attitude of their American counterparts. Ultimately, Paris threatened to sue the United States in Federal Court over the discovery of the AIDS virus which apparently took place in France (1). It was only then that the United States agreed to recognize French scientists as (co)discoverers of the HIV virus. The fact of the matter is that the virus was first discovered and isolated in France, through collaboration with American scientists, but the credit almost went exclusively to the American team.

Shortly after the publication of the 2007 study, a group of scientists put out a letter in the same journal arguing, among other things, that the epidemiology of the disease refutes the claims of the paper (32). Sure enough, it is important to remember that AIDS had killed people in Europe in the late 1970's, people who had no connections to Haiti but had traveled directly to Africa.

This second attempt at associating HIV/AIDS with Haiti follows an already established pattern reminiscent of colonial times. Haiti once again has to deal with this carefully crafted tale designed if not to make its people lose pride in the first black republic of the world but to at least perpetuate the negative image. But this does not happen only in the secular press, as we will see in the next chapter.

Chapter 8
The Lie of the Pact

On January 12, 2010, Haiti was shaken by an earthquake that killed over 200,000 by some estimates. Due to international media coverage, many people throughout the world who had no connection to Haiti or no interest in the affairs of the country became fixated on the tragedy. At the same time, they were also exposed to a religious lie that has been spread for a very long time on the first and only successful slave revolution in recorded history. I am referring to what I call The Lie of the Pact according to which the leaders of the Haitian Revolution made a pact with the Devil so they could win the independence war against France.

Since 2004, I have written several articles on the subject and have examined this religious fable from several angles. As a result, I will not repeat here in this chapter all the facts and arguments presented in these articles which are all listed and reprinted in the Appendix section of this book. Nevertheless, I think it is important to clarify a few points here and direct you to where they have been discussed already:

1.   There is no historical document or evidence of a spiritual pact with the Devil. After the success of the revolution, there was no

monument raised to the glory of Satan anywhere on the island of Haiti. Rather, the leaders of the new country started a massive nation building effort not only to protect their new freedom but also to start the long process of development (see Appendix A2). Typically when it comes to libel and slander, the abuser and the accuser are one and the same; for some reason I suspect the same cohabitation here with regards to the origin of this lie.

2. The duration of the pact is pure fiction. Out of thin air some preachers pulled down 200 years as the duration of the imaginary pact, but they made the great mistake of forgetting that people can actually count. So, let us count. If we start counting from 1791 when the general revolt started in the North, then the deal ended in 1991; and if we start from 1804 when independence was declared from France, then the deal ended in 2004. Either way, the proponents of this lie have made it impossible for them to continue using it after 1991 or after 2004. But we all know that things have not changed for the better in Haiti, which clearly indicates that the causes of the country's misery need to be found elsewhere (see Appendices A1 and A3).

3. Available historical and official documents show that the leaders of the Haitian Revolution had a strong faith in the God of heaven. They talked about God, not Satan; they built and attended churches. Henry Christophe, in particular, suffered a stroke while attending a church worship service in the city of Limonade on August 15, 1820 (33). The practical faith of

the founding fathers is discussed in detail in my 2005 article *'God, Satan, and the Birth of Haiti'* together with the general context of the Haitian Revolution (see Appendix A2).

4.   After 1804, the leaders of the new nation opened its doors to missionaries from Europe and North America and gave them the liberty to preach and teach according to their faith. Not only did the new nation adopt Roman Catholic Christianity, but protestant missionaries were regularly received in audience by presidents such as Pétion and Boyer in Port-au-Prince. The North was already receiving foreign preachers and the first recorded water baptism by immersion involving Baptist Christians took place in Cap-Haitien in 1823 (18). At the start of every New Year, the young country celebrated Independence Day on January 1 and this was the occasion to express public gratitude toward God in heaven for the success of the Haitian Revolution (34). The truth of the matter is that Haiti's founding fathers had no pact with Satan and but rather were grateful to God for his many blessings; they were concerned about human freedom in every aspect possible-including religious freedom.

5.   According to the Bible, the Devil gives riches, honor, and power to those who bow down to him and worship him. He will do it for the Antichrist (see Revelation 13; 2 Thessalonians 2:1-12), and he promised to do it for Jesus Christ during the temptation in the wilderness (see Matthew 4:8-10). Any

serious student of the Bible understands that the whole world is under the control of the evil one (see 1 John 5:19), and history shows that many rich and powerful nations of this world became prosperous through very ungodly and unjust means. Those who serve the Devil have plenty in this current age, and the Church of Satan is not made of beggars, homeless or poor people.

In reality, the people who take pleasure in invoking the lie of the pact to explain Haiti's troubles simply show how limited their understanding of the Scriptures is. When I come across such empty arguments, my mind goes back to the Book of Job and I remember what he had to go through. I have written an article pointing out some striking similarities between Job and Haiti, and it is available also here for you to review (see Appendix A4).

To me the proponents of the lie of the pact and the idea of divine curse sound like people who would have graduated with honor from FOJTI. I am sure you are wondering about the meaning of this acronym. Well, FOJTI stands for Friends Of Job Theological Institute. Of course, such an institute does not exist in real life, but the discourse of these few but very vocal ministers makes me think they would fit the profile of successful FOJTI Alumni.

This, too, Haiti has to overcome!

Conclusion

At the end of the 15th century, Haiti was visited by some irritated and greedy men from Europe who, in a few short years, turned its beautiful plains into graveyards and its creeks into streams of blood. At the start of the 19th century, Haiti stood up and reversed the deadly and destructive course of colonialism and slavery to start a new chapter in its existence.

Although Haiti is a lovely part of God's creation in the Caribbean Sea, it has constantly been the site of great challenges and power struggles. The 21st century has brought new obstacles for the country to overcome as it has to deal with the private agenda of powerful nations which, in times past, were at war with each other but now are working together to create a new world order in the context of globalization.

Haiti, once again, has the great responsibility of defining or redefining itself in terms of its priorities as a free and independent country. The nation needs to address its internal contradictions in a way that is compatible with its own laws and ideals of liberty, equality, and fraternity for all its citizens. Certainly, every social entity or religious group has a role to play in the renewal of the land because ultimately the development and prosperity of the nation will benefit everyone.

But I believe that those of us who share in the Christian faith, Haitians and as well as non-Haitians, have a double responsibility to seek the welfare of the country in very tangible ways. First, it is in the name of the Christian God that the horrific crimes of slavery were committed on the native Haitians although it is clear (I hope) that Columbus and his men were as far from Jesus Christ as the east is from the west – at least in light of the New Testament. Therefore it is our responsibility not to perpetuate the wrong but rather to do what is right as the message of Jesus Christ requires us to do. Consequently, we need to forcefully reject the lie of the pact together with the myth of the divine curse. Second, believers in Jesus Christ are commanded to love their neighbors as themselves and do good to all men. Yes, Christian churches have done good things in the country, but obviously that is not enough as the deterioration seems to continue. As one simple example, I believe that Christians alone (already several millions) can cover Haiti completely with all types of tropical trees in as little as five years, and they can do it joyfully, all for the glory of God and the betterment of the land. Such a great endeavor is not impossible at all, and Haiti can be green once again.

Certainly, Haiti can rewrite its history, change its course, and take control of its destiny to become free and prosperous once again. Nothing is impossible to those who believe, nothing is impossible to God!

Notes and References

1. Shilts, Randy (1987). And the Band Played On: Politics, People, and the AIDS Epidemic, St. Martin's Press. New York.

2. Online article published by BBC on July 14, 1989. 1989: Paris in 200-year-old revolutionary fervor http://news.bbc.co.uk/onthisday/hi/dates/stories/july/14/newsid_2503000/2503109.stm (Accessed April 09, 2012).

3. Ribbe, C. (2010). Régis Debray en Bolivie et en Haiti. Online article published in French about recent events in Haiti. http://www.tanbou.com/2010/RegisDebrayHaitiBolivie.htm (Accessed April 09, 2012).

4. Meltzer, M (1990). Columbus and the World Around Him. Franklin Watts. New York, NY.

5. Caner, E.M. and E.F. Caner (2004). Christian Jihad: Two Former Muslims Look at the Crusades and Killing in the Name of Christ. Kregel Publications. Grand Rapids, MI.

6. Clegg, L. H. II (2003). Before Columbus: Black Explorers of the New World. http://www.rense.com/general43/before.htm (Accessed March 29, 2012).

7. Hayes, F. W. III. The African Presence in America before Columbus. http://www.nathanielturner.com/africanpresenceina-mericabeforecolumbus.htm (Accessed March 26, 2012).

8. Barton, P. A. (2001). The Olmecs: An African Presence in Early America. The Perpective. http://www.theperspective.org/olmecs.html (Accessed March 28, 2012).

9. Barton, P. (2002). A History of the African-Olmecs. Race and History. http://www.raceandhistory.com/histori-calviews/04022002.htm (Accessed March 26, 2012).

10. Online article entitled 'The came before Columbus: Early Evidence of African Presence in the Americas'. http://global-blackhistory.blogspot.com/2012/02/they-came-before-colum-bus-early.html (Accessed April 06, 2012).

11. The integral text of the Constitution of 1801 is available online here: http://thelouvertureproject.org/index.php?title=Constitution_of_1801_(English) (Accessed April 07, 2012).

12. The integral text of the 1805 Constitution promulgated by Dessalines one year after independence is available here http://www.webster.edu/~corbetre/haiti/history/earlyhaiti/1805-const.htm (Accessed April 09, 2012)

13. Sankatsing, G. 2007. Development and society in the Americas. Caribbean Reality Study Center.

http://crscenter.com/DEVELOPMENT%20AND%20 SOCIETY%20IN%20THE%20AMERICAS.pdf   (Accessed April 01, 2012).

14. An online database of Haitian Literature: http://www.lehman. cuny.edu/ile.en.ile/haiti/paroles.html (Accessed April 02, 2012).

15. Guiteau, G. (2003). Le Pentecontisme en Haiti: Un Mouvement Expansionniste et Revivaliste. La Presse Evangélique. Port-au-Prince, Haiti.

16. Jeanty, E. (2011). Le Christianisme en Haiti. AuthorHouse. Bloomington, IN.

17. A 2012 online article by BBC News. Q&A: Mexico's drug related violence. http://www.bbc.co.uk/news/world-latin-amer-ica-10681249 (Accessed April 07, 2012).

18. Fantz, A. (2012). The Mexico drug war: Bodies for billions. http://www.cnn.com/2012/01/15/world/mexico-drug-war-essay/index.html (Accessed April 06, 2012).

19. Reed, L. (2008). Haiti's violent image is an outdated myth, insist UN   peacekeepers.   http://www.guardian.co.uk/world/2008/ may/11/unitednations (Accessed April 08, 2012).

20. Schaaf, B. (2001). VIOLENT CRIME IN HAITI: REALITY VS. PERCEPTION. http://haitiinnovation.org/en/2011/11/18/ violent-crime-haiti-reality-vs-perception

21. UNODC (2011). Global Study on Homicide.

http://www.unodc.org/documents/data-and-analysis/statistics/Homicide/Globa_study_on_homicide_2011_web.pdf (Accessed April 08, 2012).

22. MCCLELLAND, M. (2011). I'm Gonna Need You to Fight Me On This: How Violent Sex Helped Ease My PTSD. http://www.good.is/post/how-violent-sex-helped-ease-my-ptsd/ (Accessed April 08, 2012).

23. Valbrun, M. (2011). Haiti Made Me Do It. http://www.theroot.com/views/haiti-made-me-do-it (Accessed April 07, 2012).

24. An online article published in 2011 entitled: Haiti's Needless Cholera Deaths. http://www.nytimes.com/2011/09/07/opinion/haitis-needless-cholera-deaths.html (Accessed April 07, 2012).

25. Piarroux, R., R. Barrais, B. Faucher, R. Haus, M. Piarroux, J. Gaudart, R. Magloire, and D. Raoult. (2011). Understanding the Cholera Epidemic, Haiti. http://wwwnc.cdc.gov/eid/article/17/7/11-0059_article.htm (Accessed March 02, 2012).

26. Irin, K. R. (2011).HIV/AIDS in retreat after 30 years and 30 million deaths. http://worldandmedia.com/health/hivaids-in-retreat-after-30-years-and-30-million-deaths-0706.html (Accessed April 08, 2012).

27. Henry, W. A. III (2001). The Appalling Saga of Patient Zero. http://www.time.com/time/magazine/article/0,9171,145257,00.html (Accessed April 05, 2012).

28. The History of HIV and AIDS in America. http://www.avert.org/aids-history-america.htm (Accessed April 06, 2012).

29. Lambert, B. (1990). Now, no Haitians Can Donate Blood. http://www.nytimes.com/1990/03/14/us/now-no-haitians-can-donate-blood.html?src=pm (Accessed April 05, 2012).

30. Gilbert MT, A. Rambaut, G. Wlasiuk, T.J. Spira, A.E. Pitchenik, and M. Worobey. (2007). The emergence of HIV/AIDS in the Americas and beyond. Proc Natl Acad Sci 104(47):18566-70.

31. UNAIDS (2007). World AIDS Day 2007-Statements. http://www.unaids.org/en/resources/presscentre/featurestories/2007/november/20071128wadstatements/ (Accessed April 08, 2012).

32. Pape, J. W., P. Farmer, S. Koenig, D. Fitzgerald, P. Wright, and W. Johnson. (2008). The epidemiology of AIDS in Haiti refutes the claims of Gilbert et al. http://www.pnas.org/content/105/10/E13.full.pdf+html (Accessed April 07, 2012).

33. F.I.C. (1942). Histoire d'Haiti – Cours Elementaire et Moyen. Editions Henri Deschamps.

34. Sanders, P. (1816). Haytian Papers – A collection of very interesting proclamations and other official documents. London. Also available made online by Google at: http://www.google.ca/search?tbo=p&tbm=bks&q=inauthor:%22Henri+Christoph+(King+of+Haiti)%22 (Accessed April 08, 2012).

APPENDICES

Appendix-A1

La malédiction divine sur Haïti: un message ambigu et forcément caduc

Par Jean Gelin

gelinjr@yahoo.fr

[Publié le Mercredi 6 Octobre 2004 sur AlterPresse:

www.alterpresse.org]

J'ai lu avec soin de nombreux articles affirmant qu'une malédiction divine sur Haïti est la cause principale du malheur continu de la première république noire du monde, la deuxième république de l'hémisphère occidental après les Etats-Unis. [1] Ces textes et messages similaires diffusés à la télévision m'ont apporté un degré de malaise, non seulement en raison de leurambiguïté théologique, mais surtout à cause de la légèreté avec laquelle les données historiques disponibles sont traitées. En guise d'illustration, je reprends ici les mots d'un pasteur Haïtien bien connu : Nous pensons qu'Haïti est pauvre, non parce qu'il n'y a pas de ressources dans le pays, mais parce que nous sommes sous la malédiction de Dieu. [2]

La cérémonie du Bois Caïman, qui eut lieu dans le Nord le 14 Août 1791 sous la direction de Bookman, est citée comme le contexte dans lequel un pacte aurait été conclu entre les esclaves et le Diable pour assurer le succès de la révolution. [3] Dans l'esprit des auteurs de cette idée, il est inconcevable qu'une armée d'anciens esclaves fût en mesure de mettre en déroute les forces expéditionnaires de Napoléon Bonaparte, à une époque où pratiquement personne ne pouvait freiner l'expansion de l'empire Français. Le secours du Diable est donc évoqué pour expliquer la victoire des forces révolutionnaires Haïtiennes sur les colons et soldats français qui étaient générale-ment considérés comme de bons chrétiens. Cette considération écarte convenablement le fait que Satan lui-même est présenté dans la Bible comme le plus grand maître et marchand d'esclaves de tout l'univers. Suis-je le seul à voir l'aspect bizarre d'un tel discours?

En réponse à la prétendue participation de Satan lui-même dans le processus de libération des esclaves en Haïti, toujours selon ce même message, le Dieu des cieux aurait alors décidé de punir la jeune république en imposant sur elle une malédiction taillée sur mesure. En vertu de cette malédiction, Dieu (soutenu par sa puis-sance illimitée) œuvre constamment à maintenir la grande majorité de la population Haïtienne dans un état de sous-développement accru, d'abjecte pauvreté, et de misère chronique-d'où la descente effrénée du pays vers la destruction. Comme si l'idée même d'une malédiction divine sur Haïti n'était pas suffisante, certains auteurs vont un peu plus loin pour affirmer que ce pacte spirituel qui aurait assuré le succès de la révolution de Saint-Domingue, et sur lequel repose la totalité de cette idée, a en effet été conclu avec le Diable pour exactement 200 ans. [4] Et dans un dernier effort pour donner un peu plus de poids à leur opinion, d'autres ont cru bon de mentionner l'existence à Port-au-Prince d'une statue de porc commémorant la cérémonie du Bois Caïman. [5] Ce sont là les trois aspects fondamentaux du message.

Une telle lecture de la réalité Haïtienne me parait à la fois douteuse et dépassée. L'ambiguïté de ce message réside surtout dans le fait qu'il ne peut pas expliquer la prospérité et les progrès économiques de nombreuses nations et sociétés non chrétiennes à travers le monde, versées pourtant dans des pratiques sataniques et déshumanisantes. Sans s'en rendre compte peut-être, ceux qui véhiculent cette idée prêchent un Dieu suprême et partial, tandis que la Bible dit que Dieu juge selon l'œuvre de chacun, sans acception de personnes. [6] Sans m'étaler davantage sur la faiblesse théologique d'une telle approche, ce que j'ai fait ailleurs, [7] je pense qu'une simple analyse des données historiques disponibles suffira pour montrer que la base de ce message est tout à fait chancelante et frôle l'imaginaire.

Une statue de porc en l'honneur de Satan ? L'idée qu'une statue de porc existe actuellement en Haïti pour commémorer la cérémonie du Bois Caïman a été divulguée pratiquement à travers le monde entier grâce à des articles publiés en anglais sur le Web. Ceci a été présenté comme preuve irréfutable que la nation Haïtienne est reconnaissante envers le Diable-son bienfaiteur et libérateur. A ma connaissance, aucun de ces articles n'a fourni des photos ou des informations précises sur le lieu où se trouverait ce monument. Assurés peut-être de la crédulité de leur audience, les auteurs de ces articles n'ont pas jugé nécessaire d'offrir un support matériel quelconque à leur déclaration.

Sur la durée du présumé pacte. Dans toutes mes études sur l'Histoire d'Haïti, je n'ai jamais trouvé un seul indice relatif à la durée d'un soi-disant pacte qui aurait été conclu entre Bookman et Satan. Il y a cependant de nombreux articles sur le Web affirmant que l'alliance diabolique a été conclue pour exactement 200 ans, sans pour autant donner la source de cette précision. J'ai de sérieux problèmes avec cette exactitude pour le moins surprenante. Pour arriver à ces 200 ans, dois-je compter à partir du 14 Août 1791 ou à partir du 1er Janvier 1804, date de la proclamation de l'indépendance ? Dans le premier cas, ce pacte aurait donc déjà pris fin en 1991. Il faudrait alors trouver une autre explication pour les nombreux troubles qu'a connus le pays depuis cette date puisque la malédiction divine ne peut plus être évoquée, sa cause ayant été éliminée par l'usure du temps. Avec le second scénario, cette présumée alliance satanique aurait aussi déjà expiré dès le premier jour de l'année 2004, donnant alors libre cours à la bénédiction divine. Même le pasteur Joà« l Jeune, l'un des plus connus promoteurs de cette idée, a affirmé (selon un article publié il y a quelques années sur le Web) que le pays n'a plus un pacte avec le Diable, le contrat a été annulé, et la malédiction rompue. [8] Je souhaite vivement que les protago-nistes de la malédiction divine puissent brandir le plus vite possible une autre explication pour le prolongement de la destruction du pays. Ne la doivent-ils pas à leurs fidèles ?

Témoins de l'alliance ? Selon les documents disponibles, il ne semble pas que Bookman ait conclu aucune alliance avec le Diable avant de lancer sa révolte. Il y eut certes une cérémonie au Bois Caïman, mais ce ne fut ni la première ni la dernière rencontre de ce genre. Quiconque est habitué avec le vodou sait que les sacri-fices d'animaux constituent une partie intégrale des services, et que pratiquement tout se fait et se transmet oralement. Il n'y a donc aucun moyen sûr de savoir exactement ce que Bookman et les autres participants ont effectivement dit. Une synthèse des nombreuses traditions orales concernant la prière de Bookman est présentée à la page 43 de l'ouvrage 'Written in Blood' publié aux Etats-Unis en 1978. [9] Selon ce document, Bookman adressa sa prière au Dieu des cieux, créateur du soleil, et implora son secours ; mais il n'essaya pas toutefois d'établir un quelconque pacte spirituel.

De nombreuses tentatives d'insurrection ont échoué avant 1791, et même les premiers habitants de Saint-Domingue ont essayé vaine-ment de rompre les chaînes de l'esclavage. Cette dernière révolte aussi aurait probablement été étouffée par les Français après la mort de Bookman, n'était-ce l'entrée sur la scène du célèbre Toussaint L'Ouverture, suivi de Dessalines, Christophe, Pétion et les autres généraux qui ont commandé l'armée indigène révolutionnaire. De plus, les principes fondamentaux de liberté, d'égalité et de fraternité qui ont guidé les héros de la guerre de l'indépendance ne relèvent pas de la magie, de la sorcellerie ou de l'occultisme ; ces principes relèvent de l'essence même de notre valeur humaine, et sont tout à fait conformes à la déclaration des droits de l'homme promulguée en France vers la même époque. [10] Voilà pourquoi je trouve étrange que certains auteurs ne se soient même pas contentés d'affirmer l'existence d'un pacte satanique, mais ont eu le courage d'aller jusqu'à donner la durée exacte de ce présumé contrat. Il y a, à mes yeux, trois possibilités pour une telle connaissance : 1) ils étaient présents en 1791 comme témoins oculaires, et ont traversé deux siècles d'histoire pour apporter au monde leur témoignage authentique ; 2) ils disposent de certains documents officiels que personne d'autre n'a pu consulter jusqu'à présent ; 3) eux seuls, ils ont reçu ce message par révélation spirituelle (divine ou satanique)- auquel cas je ferais mieux de me taire pour l'instant.

Après l'indépendance en 1804, de nombreux édifices et monuments ont été érigés à travers le pays pour sauvegarder la révolution, et pour honorer la mémoire des Pères de la patrie. [11] La Citadelle du Roi Christophe est le plus magnifique de ces édifices, et fait maintenant partie du patrimoine mondial de l'UNESCO [12] comme un symbole universel de liberté. Paradoxalement, rien n'a été construit pour rendre hommage au Diable à la suite de la consommation de la victoire sur les troupes françaises, ce qui pourtant aurait été logique dans le cas de l'existence d'un pacte satanique qu'il faudrait célébrer.

A mon avis, la raison d'une telle carence est qu'apparemment personne parmi les fondateurs et premiers dirigeants de la patrie n'était au courant d'un quelconque pacte spirituel qui aurait été à la base de leur victoire militaire et politique. C'est peut-être pour combler ce vide que les prédicateurs de la malédiction ont propagé l'idée de la statue de porc. Les Héros de l'indépendance Haïtienne ont lutté pour la liberté, l'égalité, et la fraternité ; et grâce à leur union ils ont su combiner leur bravoure, expérience, intrépidité, et génie militaire pour abolir d'un seul coup l'esclavage et la colonisation dans le nouveau monde. [13] Ils ont lutté pour mettre un terme définitif à cette entreprise démoniaque et tristement mémorable qui avait pendant si longtemps déshumanisé l'homme créé pourtant à l'image de Dieu. L'oppression, l'exploitation, et l'appropriation de l'homme par son prochain ne viennent pas du Dieu des cieux, mais du Diable ; et Satan n'aurait jamais contribué à l'abolition de sa propre institution.

—————————————-

1. Leyburn, J.G. 1941. The Haitian People. Yale University Press.
2. Déclaration du Pasteur Chavannes Jeune rapportée par Andrea Garrett, For CWNews, September 5, 2003. WARFARE-Haitian Christians Seek Nation's Deliverance From Voodoo. http://www.cbn.com/cbnnews/cwn/0905   [vérifié le 6 Septembre 2004]. Propos traduits de l'Anglais par l'auteur.
3. Terry Snow. New Beginning 2004. http://www.ywam-haiti.org/features/. . . [vérifié le 6 Septembre 2004].

4. A history of Haiti and the voodoo they do. http://www.thegreat-separation.com/n. . . [vérifié le 6 Septembre 2004].

5. Brian Shipley. A brief story : Bookman-A spiritual battle. http://www.ywam-haiti.org/features/. . . [vérifié le 6 Septembre 2004].

6. Voir La Bible de Louis Segond : Et si vous invoquez comme Père celui qui juge selon l'oeuvre de chacun, sans acception de personnes, conduisez-vous avec crainte pendant le temps de votre pèlerinage (1 Pierre 1:17).

7. Gelin, J.R. 2004. La malédiction d'Haïti ne semble pas venir de Dieu.http://www.acm.ndsu.nodak.edu/ geli. . . (vérifié le 6 Septembre 2004). Cette analyse est aussi disponible gratuite-ment sous forme de livret.

8. Pasteur Joà« l Jeune via Gerry A. Seale. Haiti-God's country after a holy invasion. http://www.jesus.org.uk/dawn/1998/d. . . [vérifié le 6 Septembre 2004]. Ce rapport a également été publié à http://www.etpv.org/1998/haiti.html.

9. Heinl, R.D., Jr, and Heinl, N.G. 1978. Written in Blood-the story of the Haitian people, 1492-1971. Houghton Mifflin Company Boston.

10. Aimé Césaire. 1981. Toussaint L'Ouverture-La révolution fran-çaise et le problème colonial. Présence Africaine, Paris.

11. F.I.C. 1942. Histoire d'Haïti-Cours élémentaire et moyen. Editions NÂ° PDHG-129.

12. Le site de l'UNESCO est à http://www.unesco.org, et la page concernant la citadelle est à http://whc.unesco.org/sites/180.htm.

13. Victor, A.J. 2004. In the name of liberty-A story of Haïti (Pre-1492-1806). Linivè Kreyòl. Aussi sur le Web à http://www.ayiti-history.com.

Appendix-A2
God, Satan, and the Birth of Haiti

Jean R. Gelin, Ph.D.

© 2005, gelinjr@yahoo.fr

[Published in 2005 as a three-part article on

www.blackandchristian.com]

1-Explaining Haiti

Right or wrong, Haiti is considered the point of entry of Christianity into the New world because it is the place where Christopher Columbus built the first Spanish colony after landing on December 5th, 1492. Roman Catholicism was the official religion of Spain, and thus was imposed on all the original inhabitants of the island. The natives were made Christians by force and the island was called 'Hispaniola', meaning 'little Spain'. Before long the Indian population was enslaved and wiped out, and Africans were imported as replacements. But that's not all.

Haiti is the only place in the world where revolutionary African slaves successfully ended slavery and colonialism to build a new and independent country. All this happened when Jean-Jacques

Dessalines, his Generals, along with the indigenous army, proclaimed Haiti's independence from France on January 1st, 1804. On that day, they rejected the colonial name 'Saint-Domingue' and reclaimed the Indian name Haiti (Ayiti[1]) for the country.

In celebration of Haiti's bicentenary, the United Nations General Assembly has proclaimed 2004 the 'International Year to Commemorate the Struggle against Slavery and its Abolition'. Ironically, in that same year, several thousand soldiers from different countries landed in the country as the 'United Nations Stabilization Mission in Haiti' (MINUSTAH[2]). Two hundred years after its independence and at less than 700 miles from the coast of Florida, Haiti has become the most unstable and the poorest country of the western hemisphere. Although Haiti's free fall can easily be understood from a strictly historical perspective, religious arguments have been used by many to follow and explain the demise of this tiny nation.

Have you ever heard how some preachers or theologians try to explain the unspeakable misery that is crippling most of Haiti's population of 8 million? Everywhere you go, from your television screen to the Internet, what you are most likely to find is a reference to a spiritual pact that the fathers of the nation supposedly made with the devil to help them win their freedom from France. As a result of that satanic alliance, as they put it, God has placed a curse on the country some time around its birth[3], and that divine burden has made it virtually impossible for the vast majority of Haitians to live in peace and prosperity in their land. Surprising, right?

The satanic pact allegedly took place at Bois-Caïman near Cap-Haïtien on August 14, 1791 during a meeting organized by several slave leaders, under [Dutty] Boukman's leadership, before launching what would become Haiti's Independence War. This brutal period lasted 13 years until the last survivors of the French expeditionary forces, dispatched to Saint-Domingue with the sole purpose to re-establish slavery, were allowed by Dessalines to leave the island and return to Napoleon. Those who made it safely to France wrote and reported about the utmost bravery and supreme courage of Haiti's indigenous army.

Obviously, the idea that Haiti was dedicated to Satan prior to its independence is a very serious and profound statement with potentially grave consequences for its people in terms of how they are perceived by others or how the whole nation is understood outside its borders. One would agree that such a strong affirmation should be based on solid historical and scriptural ground. But, although the satanic pact idea is by far the most popular explanation for Haiti's birth as a free nation, especially among Christian missionaries and some Haitian Church leaders, it is nothing more than a fantasist opinion that ultimately dissipates upon close examination.

2-Exploring the religious argument

I was born and raised in Haiti, and I am a graduate of the State University in Port-au-Prince. I am also a believer in the Lord Jesus-Christ in accordance with the Bible. In all of my studies of Haitian history, however, I have yet to find a good evidence of even the idea of Satan's assistance in the Independence War, let alone a satanic pact.

For quite some time now, several articles on the Internet have mentioned the existence of an iron pig statue in Port-au-Prince as a monument to commemorate Haiti's so-called pact with the devil through Vodou. The statue would be in remembrance of a pig that was killed during the gathering by the African slaves. In an effort to know more about that rumor, I contacted several authors about the exact location of the pig statue that's incidentally nowhere to be found in the country. Their answer was complete silence, a simple apology, or just the removal of the reference from their texts.

One writer was grateful to me for pointing out the inaccuracy of her article, and she made the necessary adjustment. But I am sure that the same allusion can be found somewhere in other published pieces of writing and documents. The worst part of the whole picture is that the story is believed by many sincere Christians in America and around the world; and not only do they believe it, they also spread it as fact. The tragedy of our age is that repeated lies are often mistaken for the truth, especially when repeated long enough. That's particularly the case in religious circles where faith on the part of the audience is generally expected, but that should never be so for those who believe in the Bible.

Maybe, believers need to return to biblical texts like 1 Thessalonians 5:21, *"Test everything. Hold on to the good"*.

It's hard to know where the idea of a divine curse on Haiti following the purported satanic pact actually originated, whether from foreign missionaries or from local church leaders. In his book *"Ripe Now-A Haitian congregation responds to the Great Commission"*[4], Haitian pastor Frantz Lacombe identified a 'dependence mentality' in the leadership of the Haitian church, which resulted from the way the Christian faith was brought to the country, historically and through various denominations. Apparently, this unfortunate manner of thinking, which tends to emulate the worldview and culture of North American and European Christian missionaries, has permeated the general philosophy of the Haitian church on many levels, including church planting, church management, music and even missionary activities.

In that context, I would not be surprised if the satanic pact idea (followed by the divine curse message) was put together first by foreign missionaries and later on picked up by local leaders. On the other hand, it is equally possible that some Haitian church leaders developed the idea on their own using a theological framework borrowed from those same missionaries who subsequently propagated the message around the world. Either way, because of this message, Haiti has been portrayed as the country born out of Satan's benevolence and goodwill toward mankind. Shouldn't such a fantastic idea be tested for its historic validity and theological soundness? I invite you to take with me a closer and possibly different look at the available records.

3-A Closer Look At Bois-Caïman

The proponents of the supposed pact continuously refer to the Bois-Caïman gathering as the place where the satanic contract supposedly took place, even in the absence of solid historical evidence save their own prolific imagination. After extensive research on Haiti and several visits to the country, American writer Robert Heinl and his wife Nancy Heinl published in 1978 a volume on the Haitian revolution that deals with several aspects ofHaiti's painful history including the Bois-Caïman meeting[5]. According to these authors, Bookman sought the help of the God of heaven in his prayer, and made no mention whatsoever of a spiritual agreement with Satan. Even though the text shows Bookman was talking to the creator and not the devil, some would still contend that he could not have been really talking to God because – the way they see it-Bookman did not know God as they think they know Him.

In addition to the complete absence of any reference to Satan or to a spiritual pact in Bookman's prayer, there are two other problems associated with such an interpretation of the available records. First, those who hold that view say implicitly that God was in favor of slavery in Saint-Domingue whereas Satan himself was against it. How would they know? And how could that be? The God of the Bible created man in His own image[6], and therefore sees all men, women and children as equal in terms of their intrinsic value, regardless of their ethnicity, education or economic status. Satan on the other hand is portrayed in the Bible as a liar, a destroyer of human life, and a murderer[7]. Therefore, it is logical – at least to me-to think that God and not Satan would be in favor of ending the sufferings of the African slaves in the French colony of Saint-Domingue.

The second difficulty of that position lies in the fact that God is above all as the God and creator of all. What do I mean? The Bible contains many instances where God was involved with or answered the sincere prayers of people who were not partakers of His existing covenant but nevertheless acknowledged His existence, power and character. The supremacy and sovereignty of God is a central and undeniable truth in both the Old Testament and the New Testament. To deny this fact would be to lean toward what I call tribal theology, usually conceived or expressed in terms like these: if you are not a registered member of our church and if you do not serve and worship God the way we do, God cannot and will not answer your prayers. Those who operate under that skewed theological umbrella fail dramatically to understand that the God who said, *"You shall have no other gods before me"* (Exodus 20:3) never once said, *"I shall answer no other prayers but yours"*. David was absolutely right about God when he cried: *"O you who hear prayer, to you all men will come"* (Psalms 65:2). For those of us who believe in God we know that we belong to Him, but God Himself does not exclusively belong to us or to anybody for that matter since He created us all. As much as we are totally dependent upon God the Father for our very existence, God in contrast is totally independent of His creation, and He transcends us all.

So, when Bookman addressed his plea for help to the God of heaven, as the historical record seems to indicate, was it just pure theism? Was it a kind of simple theistic philosophy? You can debate that. But as for a spiritual pact with Satan, I have not yet seen the evidence.

Now, someone could readily ask a legitimate question about the significance of the blood shared by the participants during that unprecedented meeting. The drinking of animal blood could be easily understood in the context of a simple cultural phenomenon. Warm animal blood was routinely used as a source of strength in many ancient cultures. Even today, animal blood is consumed in many parts of Haiti, generally fried or transformed in some other way, but without any spiritual or religious connotation. It's worth recalling that this particular event took place in 1791 in rural Saint-Domingue during a gathering of malnourished, tortured, violated, abused, and terrorized men and women. The African slaves who needed their physical strength just to stay alive on the plantations found themselves in greater need of their vitality as the time of the general insurrection was approaching. It was neither the first nor the last time they had a taste of animal blood. Furthermore, as reported by the World Health Organization[8], blood derivatives and blood-based products are used by many in developed countries for therapeutic purposes, among other things.

But, if there is no good evidence that there ever was a satanic pact, and if the devil didn't play a role in the success of Haiti's revolution, who or what did? What most people have probably never

69

heard about Haiti is the real reasons the revolution was possible in the first place, 200 years ago.

4-Moving From Saint-Domingue Into Haiti

The heroes of Haiti's independence succeeded in defeating slavery and colonialism for two main reasons. First, they were united by a clear and common goal – and that's not a small thing considering the extent of the fragmentation of the colonial society. These brave men and women were united in their misery and humiliation, and that made them ready to die fighting for their common freedom rather than continue to live as mere disposable properties of the French slave masters.

Prior to 1791, there were several isolated attempts by various socio-economic or ethnic groups to bring about profound structural changes in the colony. Some wanted to escape slavery whereas others needed to maximize their profits or to reach their goals of liberty and equality with the most privileged of the system.[9] Among the Indians (native Haitians) who very early fought against slavery stands the name of Chief Henri who succeeded in building a small independent community of people living freely in the mountains. Many years later, mulattoes such as Ogé and Chavannes lost their lives trying to reach equality with the whites. At the same time, African slaves were constantly fleeing to the mountains to live freely whenever they had the opportunity to escape the horrors of the plantations in the plains. Even underprivileged and poor whites were also unhappy with the system and wanted to see significant changes that would give them greater advantages.

In the movement that followed Bois-Caïman, however, the revolting African slaves and the already free mulattoes were united in one big army with one purpose: abolish both slavery and colonialism in Saint-Domingue. With such a clear goal, their combined strength made them unstoppable. Unity among men is so powerful that even God at some point had to come down from heaven to stop a rebellious design put together by united men and women who apparently did not like the divine plan for their lives[10]. Conversely, Jesus explained what happens when unity is absent in any human institution: *"Every kingdom divided against itself will be ruined, and every city or household divided against itself will not stand"* (Matthew 12:25). It was obviously because of their intense unity that the heroes of Haiti's Independence were able to succeed. And until today, Haiti's maxim remains "L'union Fait La Force" (translated "Unity Creates Strength"). But the principle of unity itself was not the only factor for Haiti's early success.

The second reason for 1804 is that as many of Haiti's first leaders were Catholic Christians[11], they believed with all their heart and mind that it was the will of God for them to either live as free men and women or at least die fighting for their freedom. I invite you to read for yourself how these heroic men described their conditions and motives – in their own words:

God who fights for the innocent is our guide, He will not forsake us. To win or to die! There lies our motto that we will defend up to the last drop of our blood. We lack neither powder nor canons. So, Death or Liberty! May God grant it to us without the shedding of blood. Then all our wishes will be fulfilled.[12]

This is an excerpt from a letter sent to the French Governor Blanchelande who wanted to know why the slaves had revolted, as if being a slave was not in and of itself a sufficient reason. But what is interesting about the exchange is that it took place not before but after the Bois-Caiman meeting. Now, why would they claim God was on their side and guiding them, if – as the rumor goes-they had already made an alliance with the devil? It seems to me that if anybody had to know about the existence or non-existence of a satanic agreement it must have been the very people who made the deal, if such a thing ever took place. Among those who fought, bled, and died for Haiti's independence, there may have well been some who believed and practiced Vodou and others who probably had no religious faith at all and believed only in their weapons. But as for the actual leaders of the revolution, the letter says a lot about the object of their faith and the source of their strength and determination. The above excerpt clearly shows that the fathers of the Haitian revolution believed God was on their side, guiding them as the protector and defender of the innocent.

Surprisingly, those who wrote to the French had a biblically accurate understanding of God's character. Didn't God free the Israelites from slavery in Egypt[13], and didn't He deliver the young David from the giant Goliath who wanted to enslave the entire nation of Israel?[14] And after Israel had become a stable nation and the Jews began to have their own slaves (usually prisoners of war or indebted people), God himself commanded that every 7 years all slaves should be freed and all debts cancelled, in order to teach them that He was against the idea that a man could live his earthly life as the property of another man – for whatever reason. That 7th year was called the year of the Sabbath inIsrael, and after 7 sabbatical years, the year of Jubilee was celebrated on the 50th year with the same proclamation of liberty and forgiveness throughout the land.[15]

Haiti does not have a 'Liberty Bell' with a reference to the year of Jubilee stamped on it as does the United States[16], but the story of Haiti's independence has absolutely nothing to do with the devil and corresponds a great deal to these biblical principles of liberty for all men, women, and children. Decades before President Abraham Lincoln issued the 'Emancipation Proclamation' to free the African slaves in the United States[17], their brothers and sisters in Haiti had already broken their own rusty and bloody chains through unity, faith in God, bravery and determination.

In my opinion, the only story in the entire Bible that bears some good similarities with the mindset and stance of the leaders of the Haitian revolution is the story of Shadrach, Meshach and AbedNego. Like the first Haitians leaders, these young Hebrews were uprooted from their homeland, brought to Babylon (modern-day Iraq), and became human properties of king Nebuchadnezzar. While their physical body was under the King's complete control, they remained free in their spirit, their soul and their conscience. They were also supported by their strong faith in the God of their fathers, the God of Liberty, the God of forgiveness and emancipation. Therefore, when summoned by the king to bow before his statue in worship, they could do nothing but refuse. In that regard, their response was strikingly comparable to the response the Haitian leaders gave to the French-a response of unity, faith, courage, bravery and determination:

Shadrach, Meshach and Abednego replied to the king, "O Nebuchadnezzar, we do not need to defend ourselves before you in this matter. If we are thrown into the blazing furnace, the God we serve is able to save us from it, and he will rescue us from your hand, O king. But even if he does not, we want you to know, O king, that we will not serve your gods or worship the image of gold you have set up." (Daniel 3:16-18).

Shadrach, Meshach and Abednego chose death over idol worship, with the hope that God was on their side and was able to save them. Similarly, the leaders of the Haitian revolution chose death over slavery, with the hope that God, who fights for the innocent, was going to grant them their freedom and human dignity. Even if God was not going to intervene of their behalf, the Haitians leaders (like the young Hebrews before them) were ready to die rather than accept their subhuman status dictated by Napoleon. And in both cases, God's assistance was manifest for all to see. After independence, however, Haiti's leaders were faced with a new set of challenges, things they did not know and never expected.

5-Haiti's first steps after 1804

Haiti's emergence as a free nation in the New world was similar to the birth of an unwanted child. After winning its liberty through the literal destruction of the entire colonial structure, the new country was simply not welcome in the community of nations.Haiti was not needed as Saint-Domingue has been for so long in the past. The threat of invasion by France prompted Dessalines to order the construction of several fortresses throughout the country. The landmark of that campaign is the superb Citadelle, described by the world heritage committee of the United Nations as a universal symbol of liberty[18]. The invasion never materialized, and French troops did not return to the country until 200 years later under the command of the United Nations. Nevertheless, Haiti was forced to pay a large compensation to France before its independence could finally be accepted. Many historians believe that this huge financial burden, in the order of several millions and lasting one century, plays a critical role in the country's slow but steady descent into poverty.

Along with France, the United States and even the Vatican initially refused to recognize the new nation. For reasons known only to them, the leaders of the Catholic Church in Europe, who were very much involved in Saint-Domingue, declined to have diplomatic relations with Haiti, even after repeated attempts by several heads of state, and despite the fact that Catholicism was made the official religion of the new country[19].

While efforts were being made by many for international recognition and acceptance,Haiti opened its door to protestant missionaries from England and the United States shortly after 1804. These missionaries started preaching in many parts of the country, building churches, schools, clinics, and hospitals – works they still do today to the benefice of the Haitian population. But one event worth recalling is how Haiti, despite all its difficulties, made room for Jews who were fleeing Germany's persecution and the upcoming holocaust in Europe. This hospitality offered to the Jews in their time of need could be seen as yet another fundamental difference of priorities between Saint-Domingue and Haiti, considering that under the 'Code Noir' published in 1685 the presence of Jews was not tolerated in the French colonies.[20] The Jewish families that found a safe haven in Haiti around World War II formed a small and prosperous community that still exists in the country today.[21]

Although profoundly tolerant in matters of religion and faith, the Haitian people in general have always been pro-God, and open to the ideals of peace, prosperity, and freedom shared by humanity. The next time you come across the baseless and ridiculous idea that Satan himself, the greatest and most famous slave owner of the entire universe, somehow helped the Haitian revolutionary army defeat Napoleon's forces, please do yourself a big favor: Just don't believe it.

Footnotes

1. Ayiti means land of mountains in Indian language. True to its name, the country has approximately ¾ of its territory made of rugged terrains, high mountains, hills and valleys. Some have said that it was Haiti's topography along with rains and tropical diseases that defeated the French soldiers during the independence war. While it is true that the environmental conditions favored the indigenous army, with the use of guerilla warfare, the Spanish and the French were able to establish and maintain slavery on the island for 300 years under those same conditions. Therefore it is safe to conclude that nature alone was not the factor and Haiti would have never won its independence from France if the leaders of the revolutionary army were not who they were and did not do what they did the way they did it.

2. Information on the structure and mandate of the United Nations forces currently in Haiti can be found on the U.N. website at http://www.un.org/Depts/dpko/missions/minustah/.

3. Gelin, J. 2004. La malediction divine sur Haïti: un message ambigu et forcément caduc.Available online at http://www.alter-presse.org/article.php3?id_article=1766, this article in French addresses the ambiguity and abeyance of the whole divine curse idea.

4. Lacombe, F. 2003. Ripe Now – A Haitian congregation responds to the Great Commission, JoniwritrProductions. Huntington Beach, CA. Pastor Lacombe is a graduate of Moody Bible

Institute and he has recently launched a ministry aimed at encouraging Haitian believers to embrace the Great Commission.

5. A synthesis of Bookman's prayer, arranged from many oral traditions, can be found on page 43 of the book "Written in Blood-the story of the Haitian people, 1492-1971" by Heinl, R.D., Jr, and Heinl, N.G. 1978. Houghton Mifflin Company, Boston. Here is the text of the prayer: *"Good Lord who hath made the sun that shines upon us, that riseth from the sea, who maketh the storm to roar; and governeth the thunders, The Lord is hidden in the heavens, and there He watcheth over us. The Lord seeth what the blancs have done. Their god commandeth crimes, ours giveth blessings upon us. The Good Lord hath ordained vengeance. He will give strength to our arms and courage to our hearts. He shall sustain us. Cast down the image of the god of the blancs, because he maketh the tears to flow from our eyes. Hearken unto Liberty that speaketh now in all your hearts."*

6. The biblical account of the creation of man is found in Genesis 1:26-28, *Then God said, "Let us make man in our image, in our likeness, and let them rule over the fish of the sea and the birds of the air, over the livestock, over all the earth, and over all the creatures that move along the ground." So God created man in his own image, in the image of God he created him; male and female he created them. God blessed them and said to them, "Be fruitful and increase in number; fill the earth and subdue it. Rule*

over the fish of the sea and the birds of the air and over every living creature that moves on the ground."

7. Jesus talks about Satan in those terms: *You belong to your father, the devil, and you want to carry out your father's desire. He was a murderer from the beginning, not holding to the truth, for there is no truth in him. When he lies, he speaks his native language, for he is a liar and the father of lies.* (John 8:44).

8. Technical information on blood derivatives and blood-based products can be found athttp://www.who.int/bloodproducts/en/, the website of The World Health Organization.

9. See Victor, A.J. 2004. In the name of liberty-A story of Haïti (Pre-1492-1806). Linivè Kreyòl. Also on the World Wide Web at http://www.ayitihistory.com.

10. *The LORD said, "If as one people speaking the same language they have begun to do this, then nothing they plan to do will be impossible for them. Come, let us go down and confuse their language so they will not understand each other."* (Genesis 11:6-7, NIV).

11. Toussaint Louverture, among others, was known to be of the Catholic faith; when he became Governor of the island only a decade after the Bois-Caiman meeting, he proclaimed Catholicism as the religion for the land.

12. I made the translation from the original text written in French: *Dieu qui combat pour l'innocent est notre guide, il ne nous abandonnera jamais. Vaincre ou mourir! Voilà notre devise que*

nous soutiendrons jusqu'à la dernière goutte de notre sang. Il ne nous manque point de poudre ni de canons. Ainsi la Mort ou la Liberté. Dieu veuille nous la faire obtenir sans effusion de sang. Alors tous nos voeux seront accomplis. Source: Césaire, A. 1981. Toussaint Louverture: La révolution française et le problème colonial.Page 196. Editions Présence Africaine.

13. The exodus of the children of Israel from Egypt is described in the Bible in Exodus

14. The biblical story of David and Goliath can be found in 1 Samuel 17.

15. The year of the Sabbath and the year of Jubilee are described in Leviticus 25 and Deuteronomy 15.

16. Go to http://www.ushistory.org/libertybell/index.html for information on the libertyBell.

17. On January 1st, 1863, almost 6 decades after Haiti's proclaimed its independence fromFrance, President Abraham Lincoln issued the 'Emancipation Proclamation' in the United States by declaring that all persons held as slaves shall be free. Blacks were accepted into the Union Army. Seehttp://www.archives.gov/exhibit_hall/featured_documents/emancipation_proclamation/.

18. Reference to the Citadelle by the World Heritage Committee of the United Nations can be found at http://whc.unesco.org/sites/180.htm.

19. Leyburn, J.G. 1941. The Haitian People. Yale University Press.

20. The complete text of the Code Noir is available in French at http://www.haiti-reference.org/histoire/documents/code_noir. html.

21. For information of the Haiti's small Jewish community, go to the Chicago Jewish Community Online at http://www.juf.org/ news_public_affairs/article.asp?key=4870.

Appendix-A3
Can Believers Help Haiti Move From Curse Into Hope

Jean Gelin

gelinjr@yahoo.fr

[First published in 2006 on AgapePress www.agapepress.org]

Once called the "Pearl of the Antilles," Haiti has always occupied a special place among the Caribbean Islands, not only because of its beautiful landscape and rich culture, but especially for its unparalleled history. Haiti is the only place in the new world where revolutionary African slaves successfully ended slavery and colonialism to build a new country. On January 1, 1804, Haiti proclaimed its independence from France and then became the second oldest republic of the new world after the United States.

Two centuries later, the two countries stand at opposite poles in terms of stability, prosperity and wealth — with Haiti being the poorest of the entire Western Hemisphere. After episodes of foreign occupation intertwined with coup-d'états, Haiti is being led once again by a democratically elected government. On February 7, 2006, the people of Haiti elected René G. Préval as their new president. President

Préval, who ran for the party LESPWA (meaning HOPE), will govern for a period of five years in accordance with Haiti's constitution.

A Pact with the Devil?

In the midst of the country's instability, however, one segment of the Haitian society that has known a steady growth is Protestantism, since its introduction by American and British missionaries shortly after independence. As a believer myself, born and raised in Haiti, I can say that the general impact of the gospel in the country has been a positive one — considering efforts made in educational and nutritional programs, as well as in the areas of spiritual, emotional, and medical care. But one particular movement among some evangelical churches that has puzzled me is a religious campaign based on the idea that God has cursed the land to keep it from prospering because Haiti's founding fathers — among them a slave leader named Bookman — supposedly made a pact with the devil over 200 years ago.

Several years ago, however, Bishop Joel Jeune made the following statement at the end of a series of worship services and meetings that took place throughout the country:

"All Haitians now know that Haiti is no longer under any contract with Satan. The contract is canceled, the curse is broken. Praise God for His great victory!"

He went on to explain the changes expected in the country as a result:

"Already people visiting Haiti testify to a fresh atmosphere in the country. The heaviness has been lifted up. God is going to completely

change this country spiritually, economically, and socially. We now call it Haiti G.C. [God's Country]! Be encouraged with us and keep praying."

But how much truth is there in the whole satanic pact and curse message? I have researched Haiti's history and found no record that suggests early Haitian leaders ever made a pact with Satan that would bind the entire nation.

First, Haiti's constitution does not sanctify Satanism, but guarantees freedom of conscience for all throughout the land. Freedom of religion is as much real in Haiti as it is in the United States, Canada, or France. Second, there is no evidence that Bookman ever made a pact with Satan in the name of or on behalf of the entire nation of Haiti. Finally, the historical records show that Haiti's founding fathers put their faith in God during the Independence War — and not in Satan. The best evidence available for this very important point is found in a letter sent by the leaders of the revolution to a French governor. In the letter, they wrote:

"God who fights for the innocent is our guide. He will not forsake us."

If there ever was a satanic contract, those who sent the letter would have referred specifically to Satan as their leader and not to God as their guide and protector. Haiti's founding fathers knew or believed that their cause was just and God was going to help them succeed. The rest is history.

Jump to the Present

Among the candidates who lost the last presidential race stands Pastor Chavannes Jeune, who ran for L'Union Nationale Chrétienne pour la Reconstruction dhoti (UNCRH). Earlier, Pastor Chavannes, an advocate himself of the curse theory, had served as the national leader for the MEBSH (Mission Evangélique Baptiste du Sud d'Haïti), one of the country's largest Baptist organizations. As rumors started coming out about possible efforts by election officials to manipulate the results, thousands of people took to the streets to express their frustration. That's when Pastor Chavannes, who finished fourth in the race, made a statement that the Haitian people will remember for a long time:

"Christian ethics prevents me from endorsing the schemes and manipulations committed during the vote count."

Pastor Chavannes continued by saying that Haitian voters had the right to protest if they suspected that their vote was being stolen — a situation very similar to Ukraine's recent orange revolution! He also said that he would be willing to work with the new elected government for the benefit of the nation.

Now, could it be that by his active participation in Haiti's political life, Pastor Chavannes Jeune has just identified the real cause of the country's misery? Could it be that injustice, schemes, and manipulations (but not a curse from God) were all along responsible for Haiti's instability and poverty? After all, the old curse was removed about a decade ago, and Haiti's plague can no longer be examined through these defective and broken lenses.

Although many secular societies have achieved stability and prosperity through education and law enforcement, there is a strong conviction among many believers that a shared faith in God is a requirement for societal health. In the case of Haiti, the religious argument went beyond mere faith in God to include a direct involvement of the divine in the day-to-day realities of the population. The message that attempted to spiritualize the agonies of the Haitian masses places both Satan and God at the center of the debate. It's worth noting, however, that prosperous societies — secular or religious — own their stability and success to the degree of respect they have for their own laws. In that particular regard, Haiti can certainly learn from them.

Considering the lack of evidence that there ever was a spiritual contract with the devil, I wonder if the proponents of the curse theory can actually consider their work done. Now, how can believers help this ravaged little country leave the curse behind and move into a culture of hope? Maybe a strong push for law and order in Haiti should follow the religious campaign that has resulted in the cancellation of the supposed satanic pact. In the meantime, one simple thing Bible believers can always do when trying to understand Haiti's agony is to open up the Bible and read Exodus 20:16 for guidance: "You shall not give false testimony against your neighbor."

Appendix-A4
God, Satan, Job, and the Trials of Haiti

J.R. Gelin, Ph.D. © 2012

gelinjr@yahoo.fr

[Posted first on the Caribbean Reality Studies Center website

www.crscenter.com]

Beloved Haiti is one of the most abused and one of the most hated little countries on the face of the earth, at least as far as recent history can tell us. Very few countries in the world have a history as tumultuous, as disturbed and as painful as Haiti does. Over the last three decades or so this little nation has made international headlines on several occasions and most of the times in a very negative light.

In a previous article published some years ago, I established the theological fallacy of Haiti's supposed and much publicized satanic pact used by many to explain the country's seemingly never ending troubles (1). Now, I want to do something else. I invite you to follow an analogy with me and consider some unusual similarities I have found between Haiti's history and the Old Testament believer and giant in the faith called Job; I have found a pattern of satanic destruction with common elements between them.

Most people feel comfortable talking about the patience of Job, but I wonder how many would be willing to take just a sip from the cup that he drank. Likewise, almost everybody wants to discuss Haiti and even go there for some reason, from movie stars and celebrities of various sorts to singers and politicians; but I wonder how many of them would be willing to experience the sufferings of Haiti for just one week – in their own soul and in their own flesh. How many would volunteer?

Both Job and Haiti have enjoyed blessings from God prior to enduring great sufferings generated by the jealousy and wrath of the Devil. Between the life of Job and the history of Haiti, I have found three distinct but common chronological and theological periods. Let's have a quick tour.

I. The Glory Days

The first period is a period of protected glory. In the case of Job, the Scriptures say there was no one like him in the whole region due to his wealth, his fame, his justice and his spirituality; he was the greatest man among all the people of the East:

In the land of Uz there lived a man whose name was Job. This man was blameless and upright; he feared God and shunned evil. He had seven sons and three daughters, and he owned seven thousand sheep, three thousand camels, five hundred yoke of oxen and five hundred donkeys, and had a large number of servants. He was the greatest man among all the people of the East. (Job 1:1-3)

Similarly, if we consider the horrors of institutionalized slavery and the type of social and economic justice (or lack thereof) that existed in the new world up until the early part of the 19th century, Haiti is the only place where real freedom flourished for all men, women and children, regardless of ethnicity, skin color, education, wealth, or country of origin. Haiti rose up against slavery and colonialism and put a dramatic end to both systems when it declared its independence from France on January 1st, 1804. On account of the success of the Haitian Revolution, the Haitian people stood among the greatest and the most humane societies of the world during that time, and the ripple effects of this success were felt beyond the Caribbean Sea. As an example, here is an excerpt from a speech given by the great American Frederick Douglas on the immense significance of the Haitian Revolution (2). This one is relatively long but it's worth the read as it points to how a famous and well respected non-Haitian expressed his appreciation for what Haiti had accomplished with regards to the universal rights of people to be free:

Until Haiti struck for freedom, the conscience of the Christian world slept profoundly over slavery. It was scarcely troubled even by a dream of this crime against justice and liberty. The Negro was in its estimation a sheep like creature, having no rights which white men were bound to respect, a docile animal, a kind of ass, capable of bearing burdens, and receiving strips from a white master without resentment, and without resistance. The mission of Haiti was to dispel this degradation and dangerous delusion, and to give to the world a new and true revelation of the black man's character. This mission she has performed and performed it well. Until she spoke no Christian nation had abolished Negro slavery. Until she spoke no Christian nation had given to the world an organized effort to abolish slavery. Until she spoke the slave ship, followed by hungry sharks, greedy to devour the dead and dying slaves flung overboard to feed them, ploughed in peace the South Atlantic painting the sea with the Negro's blood. Until she spoke, the slave trade was sanctioned by all the Christian nations of the world, and our land of liberty and light included. Men made fortunes by this infernal traffic, and were esteemed as good Christians, and the standing types and representations of the Savior of the World. Until Haiti spoke, the church was silent, and the pulpit was dumb. Slave-traders lived and slave-traders died. Funeral sermons were preached over them, and of them it was said that they died in the triumphs of the Christian faith and went to heaven among the just.

He continued to describe what he saw in the Haitian people during his time in the country as a United States Minister representing his own country in the early part of the 19th century:

They are in many respects a fine looking people. There is about them a sort of majesty. They carry themselves proudly erect as if conscious of their freedom and independence.

As is the case for anything precious, both Job and Haiti took serious precautionary measures to guard and protect the blessings received. Job always prayed to God Almighty, asking protection and security for his children even when he was not aware of any specific wrongdoing on their part (see Job 1:4-5). Similarly, Haiti's forefathers protected the rights of the citizen to worship God freely according to their own conscience. Also, the nation took protective measures against prospective foreign enemies by building fortresses and strengthening the army. Many of these structures still decorate Haiti's landscape today, the most prominent of them all being the famous 'Citadelle' built by Henri Christophe in the North under orders from Dessalines (3).

While Job was enjoying God's blessings with his family and his estate, and as Haiti was attempting to make the most of its freedom, evil was also lurking in the shadow, ready to strike at the earliest opportunity. We read in the Scriptures that Satan specifically asked God to remove his divine protection so he could attack Job and terrorize him. By bringing his glory to the ground, Satan was hoping that Job will turn against God and curse him (see Job 1:9-11). Were that to happen, the Devil could have easily said to God that none of his creatures really love him or care about him, except when they are blessed; and in this satanic theological discourse, the Devil was looking for a justification for his own existence and his right to blaspheme against the Almighty. Unknown to him, Job was in the middle of a celestial contest whose outcome would have far reaching consequences beyond anything he could ever imagine. Can a man say yes to God no matter what? Can a man stay true to his faith after losing all he has?

For Haiti, I am not aware of any indication, information or revelation that a similar debate ever took place in heaven; but I am inclined to believe that all the wicked spiritual forces behind the slave trade took a serious blow with the success of the Haitian Revolution. As a result they would be willing to break Haiti down in order to make it renounce its own ideals of liberty, equality and fraternity. The kingdom of darkness was disturbed by Haiti's freedom and anticipated prosperity at the start of the 19th century, essentially the same way Job's spirituality and wealth bothered Satan in times past.

And all it took to put an end to the glory days was for God to allow the wicked to follow their evil desires as the inspiration of the Devil was taking shape in their dark minds and turning into actionable items. They were gnashing their teeth, perhaps drooling profusely, while looking at what could become theirs if only they could put their hands on it. Their plotting against their innocent neighbors was the beginning of the end for the first period.

II. The Testing Period

As soon as the Lord God removed the hedge of protection around Job, Satan left heaven and unleashed a relentless series of attacks against Job and his family, in order to terrorize him and force him to curse God and renounce his faith. Over ninety percent of the book of Job is dedicated to this period of intense trials. The story of Job and the last 200 years of Haiti's history point to four distinct types of assault, and together they form a satanic pattern of devastation and death.

1. It all started with foreign invasion. After Satan left heaven and went back to the earth, it became suddenly a matter of foreign policy for the Sabeans and the Chaldeans to invade Job's estate and plunder his wealth. This was done in direct violation of the 10th commandment which prohibits coveting anything that belongs to our neighbors:

You shall not covet your neighbor's house. You shall not covet your neighbor's wife, or his male or female servant, his ox or donkey, or anything that belongs to your neighbor. (Exodus 20:17)

Satan doesn't care one bit about God's commandments since he sought to dethrone him at one point in his past. The Scriptures reveal a similar pattern of disdain for God on the part of humans who work under the Devil's control to help him carry out his diverse projects of destruction and mayhem. First, the Sabeans attacked and killed the servants of Job who were in the field before taking away his flocks of several hundred oxen and donkeys:

One day when Job's sons and daughters were feasting and drinking wine at the oldest brother's house, a messenger came to Job and said, "The oxen were plowing and the donkeys were grazing nearby, and the Sabeans attacked and carried them off. They put the servants to the sword, and I am the only one who has escaped to tell you!" (Job 1:13-15)

93

Then, the Chaldeans came and formed three battalions, killed the workers, and took all the camels which were numbered in the thousands:

While he was still speaking, another messenger came and said, "The Chaldeans formed three raiding parties and swept down on your camels and carried them off. They put the servants to the sword, and I am the only one who has escaped to tell you!" (Job 1:17)

Such a detailed account of foreign aggression and damage to Haiti would be hard to compile. Why? Simply because there are too many instances where this little country was occupied by foreign military forces while posing no material threat whatsoever against the invading powers (4). In 2012 Haiti is still under foreign military control and has been for many years now. And have the invaders plundered the resources of the country or weakened its foundation during each episode? Absolutely! I encourage you to research yourself what Haiti has endured, and I guarantee that you will be amazed by what you find. For example, former American President Bill Clinton offered a public apology in 2010 for his contribution to the destruction of Haiti's agriculture while in office (5). But although profoundly devastating to the country, negative foreign intervention is only one component of the plan. The story continues.

2. Natural disasters constitute the next elements of this pattern. They came to Job in the form of lightings and building collapse, with widespread death following as the common outcome:

While he was still speaking, another messenger came and said, "The fire of God fell from the sky and burned up the sheep and the servants, and I am the only one who has escaped to tell you!" (Job 1:16)

Up to that point the children of Job were safe, and I wonder what may have been going through his mind on this tragic day as he was receiving these devastating news one after the other. But that, too, changed when he received the news of their simultaneous demise while they were feasting together in a family gathering as they have done many times before:

While he was still speaking, yet another messenger came and said, "Your sons and daughters were feasting and drinking wine at the oldest brother's house, when suddenly a mighty wind swept in from the desert and struck the four corners of the house. It collapsed on them and they are dead, and I am the only one who has escaped to tell you!" (Job 1:18)

Although death by lighting is rare in tropical Haiti, there is a strong historical record of devastations caused by flooding and earthquakes. In the evening of January 12, 2010, Haiti was devastated by a 7.5 quake that destroyed buildings and made around 200 thousand victims by some estimates, adding to the already deep level of misery that existed before for the vast majority of the people. Despite this terrible tragedy of biblical proportions (6), Haiti has never renounced its God-given right to exist as a free nation, and the Haitian people have never rejected the God of heaven in their collective theology. On the contrary, the Haitian government cancelled the annual carnival celebration and organized three days of national prayer that took place near the ruins of the devastated and collapsed national palace (7). Furthermore, church attendance increased as people turned to prayer and to God for spiritual and emotional comfort. The same way that Job did not sin by charging God of wrongdoing (see Job 1:22), Haiti as a whole has not uttered any blaspheme either, at least as far as I can tell. Let's continue.

3. Poverty and sickness came as parts of the infernal arsenal, following foreign invasion and natural catastrophes. What abject poverty could not do to Job, Satan was hoping to accomplish with sickness:

So Satan went out from the presence of the LORD and afflicted Job with painful sores from the soles of his feet to the top of his head. Then Job took a piece of broken pottery and scraped himself with it as he sat among the ashes. His wife said to him, "Are you still holding on to your integrity? Curse God and die!" He replied, "You are talking like a foolish woman. Shall we accept good from God, and not trouble?" In all this, Job did not sin in what he said. (Job 2:7-10)

Here again Job did not blame God for his adversity, and his faith remained as strong as ever. From that point on we no longer see Satan in the story or the human accomplices he found in the Sabeans and the Chaldeans. The attack on Job took a different form.

In what is yet one more point of similarity to the biblical account, Haiti is known today as the poorest country in the Western Hemisphere. Most of the people who enjoy using this description of the country do not make an effort to associate this poverty with its known historical causes, namely repeated invasions by foreign military troops coupled with regular natural disasters. It is not hard to understand that natural catastrophes alone can bring any society to its knees. But if you add regular episodes of military aggression to the equation the outcome can be easily predicted and mapped out, with also measurable negative effects on the physical health of the population. Accordingly, various diseases have afflicted part of the Haitian population, the most damaging being HIV/AIDS and the newly introduced Cholera that has already made several thousand victims (8). In all of this, Haiti continues to celebrate its national holidays as an independent and free nation (although under occupation, again), and prayers of all sorts continue to be addressed regularly to the God of heaven by a vast portion of the population.

The resilience of the Haitian people can be easily likened to the perseverance and patience of Job. But what Satan could not do to Job's spirit by using family death, poverty and sickness, his friends attempted to do with their theological speeches. Unknowingly perhaps, the friends of Job tried to break him down with their assumption that some hidden sin on his part was the real cause for his sufferings.

4. Theological injustice is the last and final type of assault. In the life of Job, the target was no longer his family members, his material

possessions or even his physical health since they were all gone. Now it was a string of verbal strikes going directly against the very fabric of this giant in the faith. The three friends of Job who came to visit him for his sufferings thought he or his children had committed some secret sin, and therefore their sudden and tragic death was justified (see Job 8:1-4; 15:4-6, 17-26; 34:31-37). They attacked his faith, his fear of God and his integrity, the three things that had made Job who he was and for which he was being tested by the Devil (in whom there is no faith, no fear of God and no integrity!). At some point during the heated theological and philosophical debate, the voice of God was heard from heaven; the Lord intervened and talked to Job, which brought him the great comfort he had been waiting for. Then God turned his attention Job's three friends and rebuked them for their errors:

> *After the LORD had said these things to Job, he said to Eliphaz the Temanite, "I am angry with you and your two friends, because you have not spoken of me what is right, as my servant Job has..." (Job 42:7)*

I am sure that by now you have already made the connection with Haiti in this analogy. The friends of Job were not able to say the right things about God because they had no idea why Job was suffering so greatly. It had not been revealed to them that the cosmic enemy of both God and man was in a campaign not only to prove to God that man (created in his image) cannot have a pure and strong love for him, but also to simply destroy Job just for the fun of it; we know that Satan comes to steal, kill and destroy (see John 10:10). In a similar way, countless friends of Haiti have attempted to justify the country's current conditions of widespread misery by invoking some secret ancestral sin (1). I wonder what God will tell them on judgment day. In the case of Job's friends, God talked to them directly because he knew them and they could hear his voice although they apparently did not seek his wisdom and counsel while visiting Job. The accusation of Job by his three friends concludes the series of attacks that characterize the testing period, and the response of the Lord introduces the third and final major segment of the story.

III. The Restoration Period

After the Lord rebuked the friends of Job, he instructed him to offer an intercessory prayer on their behalf because of their verbal sins; and after Job had prayed for his friends, God reestablished him in his health and prosperity, essentially giving him double blessings for his troubles:

After Job had prayed for his friends, the LORD made him prosperous again and gave him twice as much as he had before. (Job 42:10)

The Scriptures add that God blessed the latter part of Job's life more than the first (see Job 42:12-17). Job passed the ultimate test of faith with flying colors and stands out in the Scriptures as one of the greatest examples of patience and perseverance (see James 5:10-12). I would not be wrong to say that on judgment day Job will stand on God's side and his testimony will rise against the Sabeans, against the

Chaldeans, and against Satan. His restoration was possible because the Lord God is just, and full of compassion and mercy. As a result, he would never let the Devil terrorize his people indefinitely.

But can we expect the same for Haiti, and will the God of heaven stop the devastation to make the country prosperous again? I have no answer to this question although I am among those who pray and hope that he does. You see, this tiny nation covers approximately ten thousand square miles only, so its prosperity should be relatively easy to establish from a human and technical standpoint. In the meantime, my question to you is what role will you choose to play in the Haitian version of Job's story?

I know for sure that some people will be like Job's friends and try to elaborate on things they don't really understand, and in the process abuse and slander Haiti verbally and theologically; they seem to forget that the Scriptures teach that only the revealed things belong to us humans while anything concealed belongs to the Lord (see Deuteronomy 29:29). Others will take pleasure to participate in the satanic plan of destabilization and destruction like the Sabeans and the Chaldeans, and help to continue the devastation of the country with their actions. While no one can know for sure what is in store for Haiti, I believe you can choose what part to play in this ongoing reenactment of the age-old battle between good and evil, between faith and despair, between blessings and curses, between what's right and what's wrong. At this point in time, it is entirely up to you. What will it be?

Footnotes

1. J.R. Gelin (2005). God, Satan, and the birth of Haiti (www. blackandchristian.com)

2. A lecture given by Frederick Douglas at the Haitian Pavilion dedication ceremony at the World Fair held in Chicago, IL: http://thelouvertureproject.org/index. php?title=Frederick_Douglass_lecture_on_Haiti_(1893)

3. For a view of the Majestic Citadelle click on this link: http:// www.wmf.org/project/citadelle-henry

4. Brief outline of foreign military interference in Haiti:http://soc. hfac.uh.edu/artman/publish/article_94.shtml

5. An article on Bill Clinton's apology: http://www.msnbc.msn. com/id/35967561/ns/world_news-americas/#.Tvd7NTUV0_c

6. U.S. Secretary of State Hillary Clinton described the devasta-tion as 'biblical': http://articles.cnn.com/2010-01-18/opinion/ mcalister.haiti.faith_1_earthquake-haitian-people-haitian-war?_ s=PM:OPINION

7. Haitian President René Préval declared three days of national prayer and repentance in which he participated along with other government officials: http://www.foxnews.com/ story/0,2933,585650,00.html

8. HIV/AIDS is under control now but it has already killed thousands of people after its introduction into the country during the 1980's. Cholera was not present in Haiti prior to the arrival of MINUSTAH. Field and genetic studies have revealed that the strain causing

massive infections and death comes from a group of UN soldiers from Nepal stationed in the lower Central Plateau region: http://wwwnc.cdc.gov/eid/article/17/7/11-0059_article.htm

MAR 16 2017

CPSIA information can be obtained
at www.ICGtesting.com
Printed in the USA
LVOW12s1924241116

514316LV00001B/207/P